PURSUIT OF *Passion*

*Unlocking The Secrets to Deep Intimacy
& Lasting Fulfillment*

BY
DANNY & AMELIA COLE

PURSUIT OF PASSION

Unlocking The Secrets to Deep Intimacy & Lasting Fulfillment

Copyright © 2024 by Danny & Amelia Cole.

Build A Brother Publishing

Dedication

To God, the Father of the universe, who selected us from the very foundation of the earth to minister to marriages. Even before our parents conceived us, He called us. When we were unaware of our potential, He chose us! He chose us to speak life into struggling or faltering relationships. For this, we say, "Send us, Father, and we will go."

To our spiritual parents and marriage mentors, Dr. Creflo and Taffi Dollar: Your wisdom and guidance have been the cornerstone of our journey. Without your teachings and the strength you've imparted to us, our marriage—and our lives—would look very different today. As a matter of fact, it may not be in existence today. Your ministry has been a beacon of hope and transformation for us.

To Bishop Sidney P. Malone: Since we joined the church in 2006, your unwavering belief in us has been a source of immense encouragement. Your leadership, love, and steadfast support have been a guiding light, showing us the path even in the darkest times.

To our Vision Partners: Your physical, spiritual, and financial support has been a testament to the vision God placed in our hearts. Your love and commitment have not only affirmed that vision but have also propelled us forward in ways we could never have imagined.

And to the countless couples who have spent hours with us exploring the concept of the "Pursuit of Passion" in our relationships: We are profoundly grateful for your trust and openness. When God healed our marriage, we could never have foreseen how our journey would inspire and impact so many others. Your willingness to share in this journey has been a blessing beyond words.

Acknowledgments

We are deeply grateful to the many people who have supported us throughout our marriage. To our sister and brother, Patty and Sam Oldham, your unwavering support and encouragement have been our bedrock. This book and our marriage would not have been possible without seeing your belief in love and marriage during our darkest times.

A special thanks to our publisher, Genevieve Harris of Build A Brother Publishing, whose keen insights and meticulous attention to detail have shaped this manuscript into its final form. Thank you for sharing your wisdom and expertise and providing the support necessary to complete this manuscript.

We are particularly grateful to our mentor and coach, Clinton K. Powell, for his step-by-step guidance and belief in our Passion Pathway Program. His invaluable feedback and suggestions helped refine our ideas and improve our program.

Contents

Dedication   *iii*

Acknowledgments   *v*

Introduction   *8*

Chapter 1:

Establishing the Groundwork for Sexual Fulfillment   *12*

Chapter 2:

Building Bridges: Mastering Communication in the Bedroo *34*

Chapter 3:

Healing Emotional Scars: Navigating Past Traumas   *47*

Chapter 4:

**Deepening Connection: Enhancing Intimacy in Your
Relationship**   *65*

Chapter 5:

**Embracing Sensuality: Cultivating Pleasure in Your
Relationship**   *80*

Chapter 6:

**Integrating Growth: Mastering Your Journey to Lasting Sexual
Fulfillment**   *92*

Conclusion   *103*

References   *130*

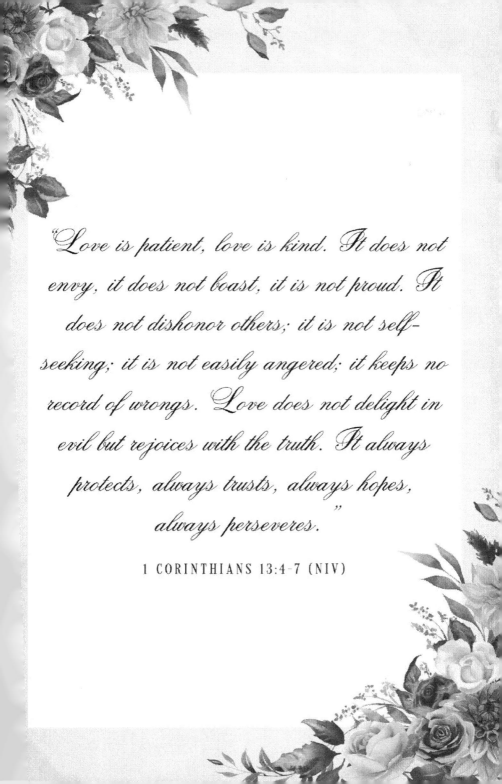

"Love is patient, love is kind. It does not envy, it does not boast, it is not proud. It does not dishonor others; it is not self-seeking; it is not easily angered; it keeps no record of wrongs. Love does not delight in evil but rejoices with the truth. It always protects, always trusts, always hopes, always perseveres."

1 CORINTHIANS 13:4-7 (NIV)

Introduction

Dear Readers,

Welcome to the "Pursuit of Passion," where we will unlock the secrets to deep intimacy & lasting fulfillment. We are the Coles, and it is our pleasure and privilege to guide you through this transformative journey. This book is not just a collection of ideas; it's a roadmap to deeper intimacy, enriched communication, and sustained joy in your relationship. Each chapter is designed to bring you closer to the love you desire and deserve.

We have crafted this book with one goal in mind: to help you and your partner build a stronger, more fulfilling relationship. Whether you're in the honeymoon phase, navigating the complexities of a long-term partnership, or anywhere in between, "Pursuit of Passion" is designed to meet you where you are. Our approach combines practical advice, actionable steps, and spiritual insights to provide a comprehensive guide for your relationship journey.

Over the years, we have worked with countless couples who felt stuck, misunderstood, or simply wanted to deepen their connection. From these experiences, we've distilled key principles that have consistently helped couples overcome obstacles and rediscover joy in each other's company. We share these principles with you in this book, along with personal anecdotes, case studies, and exercises designed to put these ideas into practice.

As you embark on this journey with us, we invite you to join the Passion Pathway Program, a community of like-minded individuals who are dedicated to enhancing their relationships. This program is an extension of the book, offering ongoing support, resources, and connections to ensure that the path you are on leads to lasting fulfillment.

We encourage you to approach this journey with an open heart and a willing spirit. Each chapter builds upon the last, creating a layered understanding of what makes relationships thrive. As you turn each page, you'll uncover new insights about yourself, your partner, and the dynamic you share. Our hope is that by the end of this book, you'll have a renewed sense of commitment, a deeper understanding of love, and practical tools to continue building a strong, passionate relationship.

Thank you for trusting us to be part of your relationship journey. Let's begin this beautiful exploration together.

With love and hope,

The Coles

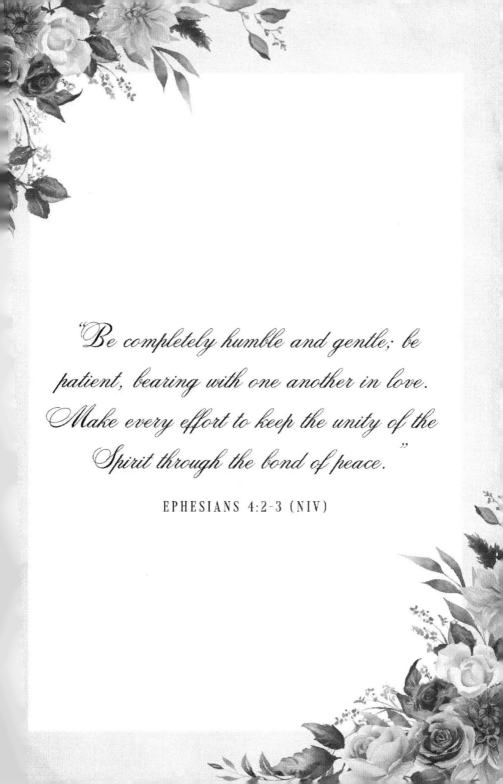

"Be completely humble and gentle; be patient, bearing with one another in love. Make every effort to keep the unity of the Spirit through the bond of peace."

EPHESIANS 4:2-3 (NIV)

Chapter 1:

ESTABLISHING THE GROUNDWORK FOR SEXUAL FULFILLMENT

Welcome to the first step on your journey toward a more fulfilling and passionate relationship. We are the Coles and so excited to embark on this transformative journey with you. We've been where you are – feeling disconnected, frustrated, and unsure of how to rekindle the spark that once burned so brightly. But through faith, communication, and a lot of hard work, we've found our way back to each other, and we believe you can too. In our experience, a fulfilling sexual relationship is built on a foundation of love, trust, and mutual respect. It's about more than just physical pleasure; it's about forging a deep and enduring connection that can withstand the tests of time and the trials of life. Our goal is to guide you through this process, helping you to break down barriers and build a relationship that is as passionate as it is profound. Sexual fulfillment isn't just about physical pleasure; it's about connection, intimacy, and love. For many couples, faith plays a significant role in shaping their beliefs and attitudes about sex. Unfortunately, misconceptions and myths about sexuality often lead to frustration and misunderstandings. We want to start by addressing some of these myths. One common belief is that sexual desire is sinful or shameful. This couldn't be further from the truth. Sexuality is a beautiful, God-given gift meant to bring joy and deepen the bond between husband and wife.

Let's delve into some common misconceptions and their impacts on relationships. One prevalent myth is that "good" Christians should not talk openly about sex. This belief can create a barrier to honest communication, leading to misunderstandings and unmet needs. It's essential to recognize that open, respectful dialogue about sex is a crucial component of a healthy relationship. Another myth is that sexual desire diminishes naturally over time and that this is just something couples must accept. While it's true that the intensity of sexual desire can fluctuate, it doesn't mean that passion has to fade. Understanding the natural ebb and flow of desire can help couples remain patient and compassionate with each other.

For many, faith is the cornerstone of their lives, influencing decisions, actions, and beliefs. When it comes to sexuality, faith can offer a framework for understanding and celebrating this aspect of our humanity. Embracing your faith's teachings about love, respect, and intimacy can enrich your sexual relationship, making it a source of joy and connection rather than frustration. In our journey, we've found that viewing sex as a sacred act – a way to express love and devotion – has transformed our perspective. It's not just about the physical act; it's about what it represents: unity, love, and the divine connection between husband and wife.

Practical Steps to building a strong foundation for sexual fulfillment

Before we explore deeper the misconceptions, let's focus on practical steps to build a strong foundation for sexual fulfillment. These steps are designed to help you and your spouse reconnect on multiple levels, fostering intimacy and understanding. Open, honest communication is the bedrock of a healthy sexual relationship. Talking about your needs, desires, and concerns without fear of judgment or rejection is essential. Here are some tips for effective communication:

1. Create a Safe Space: Ensure that Both Partners Feel Safe to Express Themselves

Creating a safe space in your relationship is fundamental for fostering open and honest communication. When both partners feel secure and respected, they are more likely to express their thoughts, feelings, and desires without fear of judgment or reprisal. This sense of safety is essential for building trust and intimacy. One of the key elements of creating a safe space is active listening without interruption. When your partner is speaking, give them your full attention. This means putting aside distractions, making eye contact, and focusing on what they are saying. Avoid the urge to interrupt, even if you have something important to add or a different perspective. Interrupting can make your partner feel unheard and disrespected, which can shut down open communication.

Responding with empathy and understanding is equally important. Empathy involves putting yourself in your partner's shoes and trying to understand their feelings and perspectives. When your partner shares something with you, acknowledge their emotions and validate their experiences. Phrases like "I can see how that would be really difficult for you" or "I understand why you feel that way" can go a long way in making your partner feel heard and supported.

Another critical aspect of a safe space is ensuring that your relationship is a judgment-free zone. This means accepting your partner's thoughts and feelings without criticism or judgment. Everyone has unique experiences and perspectives, so respecting those differences is important. When your partner feels that they can share anything with you without being judged, it strengthens the bond of trust and encourages more open communication.

Establishing and respecting boundaries is also vital for creating a safe space. Each partner should feel comfortable setting boundaries about what they are willing to discuss and how they want to be treated. Respecting these boundaries shows that you value your partner's comfort and autonomy. For instance, if your partner needs time to process their thoughts before discussing a sensitive issue, respect that need and give them the space they require.

Creating a safe space also involves encouraging vulnerability. Vulnerability is the willingness to show your true self, including your fears, insecurities, and desires. When both partners feel safe to be vulnerable, it deepens the emotional connection and fosters a stronger bond. Share your own vulnerabilities with your partner and encourage them to do the same. This mutual openness can create a more profound understanding and connection between you.

Patience and compassion are essential components of a safe space. Understand that opening up and expressing oneself can be challenging, especially if past experiences have made your partner wary of vulnerability. Be patient with each other as you navigate these conversations, and show compassion for your partner's struggles. This supportive approach will help build a more trusting and intimate relationship.

Creating a safe space in your relationship involves active listening, empathetic responses, maintaining a judgment-free zone, setting and respecting boundaries, encouraging vulnerability, and practicing patience and compassion. Fostering a secure and respectful environment facilitates open and honest communication, strengthens your emotional connection, and builds a more fulfilling and intimate relationship.

2. Be Honest and Direct: Don't Beat Around the Bush

Honesty and directness are essential for effective communication in a relationship. Being clear and straightforward about your needs, desires, and concerns can prevent misunderstandings, reduce resentment, and build a stronger connection with your partner. Here are several strategies for practicing honesty and directness in your relationship.

Clarity in communication ensures that both partners understand each other's perspectives and needs. When you express yourself clearly and directly, it eliminates ambiguity and leaves little room for misinterpretation. This is particularly important when discussing sensitive or complex issues, as misunderstandings can lead to unnecessary conflict and frustration. When expressing your needs and desires, it's crucial to be specific and concrete. Instead of vague statements like "I want more attention," be precise about what you need. For example, you might say, "I would love it if we could spend at least one evening a week having dinner together without distractions." This specificity helps your partner understand exactly what you are looking for and how they can meet your needs.

Addressing concerns directly and respectfully is another important aspect of honest communication. If something is bothering you, don't keep it bottled up. Holding onto grievances can lead to resentment and distance in the relationship. Instead, bring up your concerns calmly and respectfully. Use neutral language and focus on how the issue affects you rather than blaming your partner. For example, instead of saying, "You never help with the chores," try, "I feel overwhelmed when I have to handle all the chores by myself."

Passive-aggressive behavior, such as giving the silent treatment or making indirect comments, is counterproductive and can damage your relationship. Confronting issues head-on is essential rather than resorting to indirect or manipulative tactics. Being honest and direct means facing problems openly and working together to find solutions.

Transparency is a cornerstone of trust in a relationship. Being open and honest about your thoughts, feelings, and actions helps build trust and reinforces your commitment to the relationship. If you've made a mistake or if something is bothering you, be upfront about it. Hiding the truth or being deceitful can erode trust and create a rift between you and your partner.

Assertiveness is about standing up for your own needs and rights while respecting those of your partner. It involves expressing yourself confidently and clearly without being aggressive or dismissive.

Practicing assertiveness can help you communicate your needs effectively and foster mutual respect in your relationship. Techniques like using "I" statements, maintaining eye contact, and speaking in a calm and steady tone can enhance your assertiveness skills.

Setting aside regular time for honest conversations can help ensure that both partners have the opportunity to express themselves. This might be a weekly check-in where you discuss your feelings, needs, and any issues that have arisen. Regular communication helps prevent small issues from escalating into larger conflicts and keeps both partners aligned.

Difficult conversations are inevitable in any relationship. When addressing sensitive topics, approach the conversation with empathy and a willingness to listen. Acknowledge your partner's feelings and perspectives, and be prepared to compromise. Remember that the goal is to find a resolution that works for both of you, not to "win" the argument.

Being honest and direct in your relationship involves clear and specific communication, addressing concerns respectfully, avoiding passive-aggressive behavior, building trust through transparency, practicing assertiveness, creating a routine for honest conversations, and handling difficult conversations with empathy. Adopting these strategies fosters open and effective communication, strengthens your connection, and builds a more fulfilling and harmonious relationship.

3. Practice Active Listening: Fully Engaging with Your Partner

Active listening is a vital skill for effective communication in relationships. It goes beyond simply hearing the words your partner is saying; it involves fully engaging with their message, showing that you value their feelings and opinions. Active listening fosters mutual understanding, reduces conflicts, and strengthens emotional connections. Here's how to practice active listening in your relationship.

The first step in active listening is giving your partner your undivided attention. This means putting away distractions such as phones, laptops, or televisions. Make eye contact, face your partner, and focus entirely on what they are saying. Doing this shows that their words and feelings are important to you.

Reflective listening involves paraphrasing your partner's words to ensure you understand their message correctly. For example, if your partner says, "I feel like you don't appreciate what I do around the house," you might respond with, "It sounds like you're feeling unappreciated for your efforts at home." This technique helps clarify your partner's message and demonstrates that you are actively engaged in the conversation.

Validation is a crucial component of active listening. It involves acknowledging and affirming your partner's feelings, even if you don't fully agree with their perspective. Validation can be as simple as saying, "I can see why you would feel that way," or "That must be really hard for you." By validating your partner's emotions, you show empathy and support, which can help de-escalate tensions and build trust.

Open-ended questions encourage your partner to share more about their thoughts and feelings. Instead of asking questions that can be answered with a simple "yes" or "no," ask questions that require more elaboration. For example, "How did that make you feel?" or "Can you tell me more about what happened?" These questions show that you are interested in understanding their experience more deeply.

Interrupting your partner while they are speaking can make them feel disrespected and unheard. Practice patience by allowing them to finish their thoughts before you respond. Even if you feel the urge to interject, remind yourself that listening fully is more important than getting your point across immediately.

Nonverbal cues such as nodding, maintaining eye contact, and leaning slightly forward can convey that you are actively listening. These gestures show that you are engaged and interested in what your partner is saying. Be mindful of your body language, as it can significantly impact how your partner perceives your level of engagement.

At the end of the conversation, summarizing the main points and asking for clarification if needed can ensure mutual understanding. For example, you might say, "So, I'm hearing that you feel unappreciated when I don't acknowledge your efforts. Is that correct?" This summary helps confirm that you have accurately understood your partner's message and provides an opportunity for any necessary clarifications.

When it's your turn to respond, do so thoughtfully and respectfully. Address your partner's concerns directly and offer your perspective without dismissing their feelings. Use "I" statements to express your thoughts and feelings, and avoid making accusatory or defensive comments.

Empathy is the ability to understand and share the feelings of another person. Practicing empathy involves putting yourself in your partner's shoes and trying to see the situation from their perspective. This empathetic approach can deepen your connection and foster a more compassionate and supportive relationship.

Practicing active listening involves giving full attention, reflective listening, validating emotions, asking open-ended questions, avoiding interruptions, showing nonverbal engagement, summarizing and clarifying, responding thoughtfully, and practicing empathy. Mastering these techniques can enhance your communication skills, foster mutual understanding, and strengthen your emotional bond with your partner.

4. Use "I" Statements: Express Your Feelings and Needs

Using "I" statements is a powerful communication technique that helps express your feelings and needs without sounding accusatory. This approach fosters a more positive and productive dialogue, reduces defensiveness, and promotes mutual understanding in relationships. Here's how to effectively use "I" statements and why they are important. "I" statements focus on your feelings and experiences rather than blaming or criticizing your partner. They typically follow a structure that includes three components:

1. A description of the behavior or situation.
2. The feelings you experienced as a result.
3. The impact the behavior had on you or what you need.

For example, instead of saying, "You never listen to me," an "I" statement would be, "I feel unheard when I'm talking and you look at your phone." One of the key benefits of using "I" statements is that they help reduce defensiveness. When you frame your concerns in terms of your own experiences, it is less likely to come across as an attack. This makes it easier for your partner to listen to your perspective without feeling the need to defend themselves. For instance, saying, "I feel hurt when our plans change last minute," is less confrontational than "You always ruin our plans." "I" statements encourage personal responsibility for your feelings and actions.

By focusing on your own experiences, you acknowledge that your emotions are your own, and not solely the result of your partner's behavior. This can foster a sense of empowerment and accountability in the relationship. For example, "I feel anxious when our finances are tight, and I need us to discuss our budget together" takes ownership of your feelings and suggests a collaborative solution. Using "I" statements can enhance clarity in communication. They help you articulate your feelings and needs more precisely, which can prevent misunderstandings.

Clear communication is essential for resolving conflicts and strengthening your relationship. For example, "I feel appreciated when you help with the chores" clearly communicates what makes you feel valued. Expressing your feelings openly and honestly can build emotional intimacy in your relationship. When you use "I" statements, you share a part of yourself with your partner, which can deepen your connection and understanding of each other. This vulnerability fosters a sense of closeness and trust.

Examples of "I" Statements

To illustrate how "I" statements can be used in different situations, here are a few examples:

- Instead of "You never spend time with me," try "I feel lonely when we don't spend time together."

- Instead of "You always interrupt me," try "I feel frustrated when I'm interrupted because I want to feel heard."

- Instead of "You don't care about my opinions," try "I feel valued when my opinions are considered in our decisions."

Incorporating "I" statements into your daily communication takes practice. Start by paying attention to how you express your feelings and needs. When you catch yourself using a "you" statement, try reframing it as an "I" statement. With time and practice, this approach will become more natural and intuitive. Encourage your partner to use "I" statements as well. When both partners adopt this communication style, it can significantly improve the quality of your interactions. It creates a more supportive and understanding environment where both partners feel heard and respected. Even with the best intentions, your partner sometimes might react defensively. Stay calm and reaffirm your commitment to using respectful and non-accusatory language when this happens. Encourage your partner to share their feelings using "I" statements, and approach the conversation with empathy and an open mind.

Using "I" statements is an effective communication technique that promotes clarity, reduces defensiveness, enhances emotional intimacy, and fosters personal responsibility. By expressing your feelings and needs in a non-accusatory way, you can create a more positive and productive dialogue in your relationship. Practice this approach regularly, encourage mutual use, and handle reactions with empathy to strengthen your connection and improve communication with your partner.

It's time to tackle those myths head-on.

Take a moment to write down any beliefs about sex that you've carried with you. These might be things you were taught growing up, messages from society, or even misconceptions you've internalized over time. Once you've written them down, ask yourself: Are these beliefs helping or hindering our connection? Are they rooted in love and understanding or fear and misinformation?

Reflecting on these questions can be the first step in breaking down barriers and opening up new avenues for intimacy. Journaling can be a powerful tool for self-discovery and growth. Take some time to write about your personal beliefs and attitudes towards sexuality. How do these beliefs align with your faith? How have they shaped your relationship? Be honest and open with yourself; remember, this is a judgment-free zone.

Here are some prompts to get you started:

- How do I feel about my sexuality?

- What messages about sex did I receive growing up?

- How do these messages impact my relationship with my spouse?

- What changes would I like to make in my beliefs about sex?

One of the most valuable aspects of this program is the private online community you'll be joining. Our online virtual classes are accessible around the clock, every day of the week, allowing you to watch them at your convenience. Plus, you're not alone in this journey. Every couple here is working towards the same goal: a more passionate, fulfilling relationship.

In our private online community, we encourage you to participate in the weekly group sessions. Share your experiences, offer support, and lean on each other. There is strength in numbers; together, we can achieve incredible things. In our journey, we found that connecting with other couples facing similar struggles incredibly empowering. Sharing your experiences and hearing others' stories can provide new insights and perspectives. It can also help you realize that you're not alone in your struggles, which can be immensely reassuring. Our weekly group sessions are designed to foster a sense of community and provide ongoing support. These sessions are a safe space to share your thoughts, ask questions, and encourage others. By building these connections, you'll create a network of support that extends beyond this program. Most couples that we work with say that by the end of the first week, they feel a renewed sense of awareness and openness. Understanding the impact of faith and culture on your sexual frustration is the first step toward overcoming it. Embrace new perspectives and be willing to challenge old beliefs. Remember, this is a journey; every step you take brings you closer to a deeper, more fulfilling connection with your spouse.

It's important to celebrate the small victories along the way. Maybe you had a difficult conversation that you've been avoiding, or perhaps you learned something new about your partner's desires. These moments of growth are significant and should be acknowledged and celebrated. As we move forward, set some specific goals for your relationship. These could be related to improving communication, increasing physical intimacy, or exploring new ways to connect emotionally. Clear goals will give you a sense of direction and purpose, helping you stay motivated and focused on your journey. Thank you for trusting us with your hearts and your journey. We're honored to be a part of it and can't wait to see the incredible growth and transformation that lies ahead. Remember, this is just the beginning. Your steps now will lay the groundwork for a more passionate, fulfilling, and deeply connected relationship.

A Message from the Coles

We believe that every couple has the potential to experience profound love and intimacy. It takes effort, patience, and a willingness to grow, but the rewards are immeasurable. We've been through the ups and downs, and we know that with faith and commitment, anything is possible.

As you embark on this transformative journey with passion, remember this is only the beginning. As we introduce you to the foundational principles that will guide your relationship renewal, we invite you to consider joining the Passion Pathway Program. This program is designed to offer you continuous support and deeper insights as you and your partner rediscover each other and lay the groundwork for lasting fulfillment. Take this first step with confidence by joining our private online community, and know that you are supported every step of the way. Together, we will break down barriers, build new foundations, and create a passionate, fulfilling, and everlasting love.

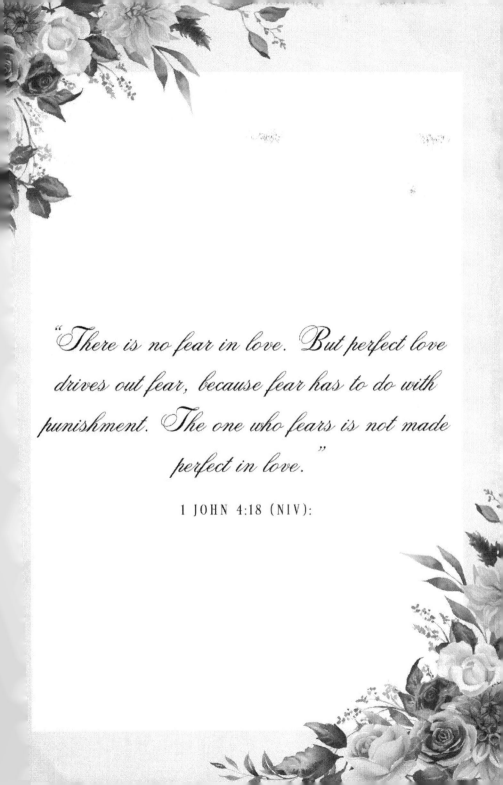

"There is no fear in love. But perfect love drives out fear, because fear has to do with punishment. The one who fears is not made perfect in love."

1 JOHN 4:18 (NIV):

Chapter 2:

BUILDING BRIDGES: MASTERING COMMUNICATION IN THE BEDROOM

*W*elcome to Chapter 2 of our journey towards a more fulfilling and passionate relationship. In this chapter, we will explore the essential role of communication in the bedroom. Through our own experiences, we have learned that open, honest, and empathetic communication is the cornerstone of a healthy and satisfying sexual relationship. It's not just about expressing your desires and needs; it's about creating a deeper connection and understanding between you and your partner.

In this chapter, we will delve into the importance of effective communication in the bedroom, discuss common barriers and some strategies for overcoming common barriers, and provide practical, actionable steps to enhance your ability to communicate effectively with your partner about your sexual needs and desires.

Effective Communication in the Bedroom

Effective communication is vital in every aspect of a relationship, and the bedroom is no exception. For many couples, discussing sexual needs and desires can be intimidating or uncomfortable. However, open communication about sex can significantly enhance intimacy, trust, and satisfaction in your relationship. Silence about sexual matters can lead to misunderstandings, unmet needs, and feelings of dissatisfaction or resentment. It's essential to break the silence and start having honest conversations about your sexual relationship. This doesn't mean you have to have a formal "sex talk" every week, but it does mean being open and willing to discuss your feelings, desires, and concerns as they arise. When you communicate openly and honestly about your sexual needs and desires, it builds trust and intimacy between you and your partner. It shows that you respect each other enough to be vulnerable and honest. This level of openness can create a deeper emotional connection, enhancing physical intimacy.

Studies have shown that couples who communicate effectively about sex tend to have higher levels of sexual satisfaction. When you and your partner are on the same page about what you like, what you don't like, and what you want to try, it leads to a more fulfilling sexual experience for both of you. Before we dive into the strategies for improving communication, it's important to recognize some common barriers that couples face when discussing sexual matters.

Common Barriers

Many people fear that expressing their sexual desires or concerns will lead to judgment or rejection from their partner. This fear can prevent open and honest communication, leading to unmet needs and dissatisfaction. Feelings of shame or embarrassment about sex can also be significant communication barriers. These feelings might stem from cultural or religious beliefs, past experiences, or societal attitudes about sex. A lack of confidence in one's sexual abilities or body image can make it difficult to discuss sexual needs and desires. This can lead to a reluctance to initiate conversations about sex. Assumptions and misunderstandings about your partner's wants or needs can also hinder effective communication. It's important to approach these conversations with an open mind and a willingness to listen.

Strategies for Overcoming Barriers to Master Communication in the Bedroom

Now that we've identified some common barriers, let's explore strategies for overcoming them and mastering communication in the bedroom. As discussed in Chapter 1, some strategies include creating ground rules for a safe and comfortable environment, being honest and direct, practicing active listening, and using "I" statements. In addition, we will discuss exploring and experimenting together and addressing sexual issues or concerns.

1. Creating a Safe and Comfortable Environment

Creating a safe and comfortable environment is crucial for effective communication. Here are some ground rules. Ensure that both partners feel safe to express themselves without fear of judgment or rejection. Choose a time and place where you both feel relaxed and comfortable. Avoid discussing sensitive topics when you are stressed, tired, or distracted. A quiet, private space where you won't be interrupted is ideal. Agree to listen without interrupting, speak from your own perspective, and avoid blame or criticism. Establishing ground rules will ensure your conversations remain respectful and productive. Establishing ground rules will also help create a safe space for open communication.

Being Honest and Direct

Another strategy is honesty and directness, which are essential for effective communication about sex. Be clear and specific about your needs, desires, and concerns. When expressing your desires, be specific about what you want. Instead of saying, "I want more intimacy," try saying, "I would love it if we could cuddle more often after sex." This clarity helps your partner understand exactly what you need. If something is bothering you, address it directly but respectfully. Use "I" statements to express your feelings without sounding accusatory. For example, instead of saying, "You never initiate sex," say, "I feel undesired when I'm always the one initiating sex."

Practice Active Listening

Active listening is a vital component of effective communication. It involves fully engaging with what your partner is saying and showing that you value their feelings and opinions. Reflective listening involves paraphrasing your partner's words to ensure you understand their message correctly. For example, if your partner says, "I feel like we don't spend enough time on foreplay," you might respond with, "It sounds like you would like us to spend more time on foreplay. Is that right?"

Using "I" Statements

Validation involves acknowledging and affirming your partner's feelings, even if you don't fully agree with their perspective. This can be as simple as saying, "I understand why you feel that way," or "That must be really frustrating for you." Using "I" statements helps express your feelings and needs without sounding accusatory. This approach fosters a more positive and productive dialogue. Here are some examples of how to reframe common concerns as "I" statements:

Instead of "You never spend time with me," say, "I feel lonely when we don't spend time together."

Instead of "You always interrupt me," say, "I feel frustrated when I'm interrupted because I want to feel heard."

Instead of "You don't care about my opinions," say, "I feel valued when my opinions are considered in our decisions."

Exploring and Experimenting Together

Exploring and experimenting together can be a fun and effective way to enhance your sexual relationship. This involves being open to trying new things and discovering what brings both of you pleasure. Have an open conversation about your fantasies and desires. This can be an exciting way to learn more about each other's sexual preferences and interests. Approach this conversation with curiosity and an open mind, and be willing to share your fantasies as well. Be willing to try new things together. This might involve exploring new sexual activities, trying different positions, or experimenting with sex toys. The key is approaching these experiences with a sense of adventure and a willingness to learn and grow together.

Addressing Sexual Issues and Concerns

Addressing sexual issues and concerns openly and honestly is crucial for maintaining a healthy sexual relationship. This might involve discussing problems such as mismatched libidos, sexual dysfunction, or other challenges. If you're facing persistent sexual issues that you can't resolve on your own, don't hesitate to seek professional help. A sex therapist or counselor can provide valuable insights and strategies for overcoming these challenges. Be patient and compassionate with each other as you work through these issues. Remember that sexual problems are common and can be addressed with the right approach and support.

Practical Steps and Exercises to Enhance Sexual Communication

Now that we've discussed the importance of communication, common barriers, and strategies for improving them, let's look at some practical steps and exercises you can implement to enhance your sexual communication.

Identifying Your Communication Styles

Start by identifying your individual communication styles. Take some time to reflect on how you typically communicate and how this affects your interactions with your partner. Consider discussing these reflections with your partner to understand each other's communication styles better.

Role-Playing Scenarios

Role-playing scenarios can be a fun and effective way to practice expressing your sexual needs and desires in a safe and supportive environment. Choose a scenario where one partner expresses a desire or concern, and the other practices active listening and responding with empathy and understanding.

Create an Intimacy Inventory

Create an intimacy inventory to reflect on different aspects of intimacy within your relationship. This might include emotional intimacy, physical intimacy, and sexual intimacy. Use this inventory to identify areas where you are strong and areas where you would like to improve.

Plan a Sensual Exploration Date

Plan a sensual exploration date to engage in sensory activities that heighten awareness of sensual pleasure. This might involve giving each other massages, exploring different textures and sensations, or simply spending time touching and connecting without the pressure of intercourse.

Schedule Regular Check-Ins

Schedule regular check-ins to discuss your sexual relationship and address any concerns or needs that may arise. These check-ins can be a valuable opportunity to ensure both partners feel heard and supported.

Conclusion

In this chapter, we discussed the importance of effective communication in the bedroom, some common barriers and strategies for overcoming those barriers, and practical, actionable steps to enhance your ability to communicate effectively with your partner about your sexual needs and desires.

Effective communication in the bedroom is essential for a healthy and satisfying sexual relationship. By creating strategies for a safe and comfortable environment, being honest and direct, practicing active listening, using "I" statements, exploring and experimenting together, and addressing sexual issues and concerns, you can enhance your ability to communicate effectively with your partner about your sexual needs and desires.

There are also some practical steps and exercises you can implement to enhance your sexual communication, such as identifying your communication styles, role-playing scenarios, creating an intimacy inventory, planning a sensual exploration date, and scheduling regular check-ups. Remember, this journey is about building bridges and deepening your connection with your partner. You can create a more fulfilling and passionate relationship with patience, empathy, and a willingness to grow.

A Message from the Coles

We hope this chapter has provided valuable insights and practical strategies for mastering communication in the bedroom. As you continue on this journey, remember that open and honest communication is the key to a deeper and more satisfying connection with your partner.

Having established a solid foundation for sexual fulfillment in your relationship, why not deepen your exploration and understanding by joining the Passion Pathway Program? Each step in this chapter is a step toward deeper connection, and the program is here to guide you through these steps, offering personalized support and community interaction that enriches your journey toward a truly fulfilling partnership. Embrace the process, be patient with each other, and celebrate the progress you make together.

"And over all these virtues put on love, which binds them all together in perfect unity."

COLOSSIANS 3:14 (NIV)

Chapter 3:

HEALING EMOTIONAL SCARS: NAVIGATING PAST TRAUMAS

W elcome to Chapter 3 of our journey towards a more fulfilling and passionate relationship. This chapter will explore the sensitive and often challenging topic of healing emotional scars and navigating past traumas. We understand how past experiences can cast long shadows over your present relationship, affecting your ability to connect and communicate. Our goal is to provide you with the tools and support you need to address these issues, heal together, and build a stronger bond.

Trauma can take many forms—whether it's related to previous relationships, childhood experiences, or specific incidents within your current partnership. Healing these wounds requires patience, empathy, and a commitment to working through the pain together. In this chapter, we'll guide you through the process of identifying and addressing these traumas, offering practical steps to help you and your partner move forward and practical exercises you can implement to facilitate healing and strengthen your relationship.

Identifying and Addressing Traumas

Emotional scars and traumas are often deeply rooted in our past, influencing our behavior, thoughts, and feelings in the present. These experiences can create barriers to intimacy and trust, making it difficult to open up to your partner fully. Recognizing and understanding these traumas is the first step toward healing.

Trauma can manifest in various ways within a relationship. Some common effects include:

- Trust Issues: Past betrayals or abuses can make it difficult to trust your partner fully.

- Communication Barriers: Trauma can hinder your ability to express your feelings and needs openly.

- Emotional Distance: You might struggle to connect emotionally, leading to feelings of isolation.

- Triggers and Flashbacks: Certain situations or behaviors might trigger painful memories, causing distress.

Understanding how these issues affect your relationship is crucial for addressing them effectively. It's important to approach these challenges with compassion and a willingness to work together toward healing. The first step in healing is to identify the traumas affecting your relationship. This might involve reflecting on your experiences and discussing them with your partner. Remember, this process can be emotionally intense, so it's important to proceed with care and support each other. Take some time to reflect on your past experiences and how they have shaped your current behaviors and feelings. Consider journaling your thoughts and emotions to gain a deeper understanding of your traumas. Here are some questions to guide you:

- What past experiences have left emotional scars?

- How do these experiences affect your relationship today?

- What triggers emotional pain or distress in your relationship?

Once you've reflected on your experiences, have an open and honest conversation with your partner. Share your reflections and listen to their experiences as well. This dialogue can help you both understand each other's struggles and provide a foundation for mutual support.

Practical Steps to Help You and Your Partner Move Forward

Healing emotional scars and navigating past traumas is a gradual process that requires dedication and patience. Here are some actionable steps to help you and your partner on this journey.

Step 1: Creating a Safe Space for Healing

Creating a safe space is essential for addressing trauma. This involves establishing an environment where both partners feel secure and supported. Set clear boundaries to ensure that both partners feel safe during discussions about trauma. Agree on topics that are off-limits or that require special sensitivity. Respecting these boundaries can help create a trusting and supportive environment. Empathy is crucial when discussing past traumas. Try to understand your partner's perspective and validate their feelings. Phrases like "I can see how that would be really difficult for you" or "I understand why you feel that way" can make a significant difference. Reassurance is important when dealing with trauma. Remind your partner that you are there for them and committed to working through these issues together. This reassurance can help build trust and security.

Step 2: Journaling and Reflecting

Journaling can be a powerful tool for processing emotions and gaining insight into your experiences. Encourage both partners to keep a journal to explore their thoughts and feelings. Encourage each partner to spend time journaling about their experiences and emotions. This can help clarify thoughts and provide a safe outlet for expressing difficult feelings. Here are some journal prompts to get started:

- What emotions do you feel when thinking about past traumas?

- How do these emotions affect your relationship?

- What steps can you take to address these emotions?

If comfortable, share some of your journal entries with your partner. This can foster understanding and empathy and provide a basis for discussing how to support each other through the healing process.

Step 3: Practicing Forgiveness

Forgiveness is a critical component of healing. This involves letting go of resentment and anger towards those who have hurt you and forgive yourself for any perceived shortcomings or mistakes. Engage in a forgiveness practice to help release negative emotions. This might involve mindfulness exercises, prayer, or meditative practices focused on forgiveness. Here is a simple exercise to try:

1. Find a quiet space where you can sit comfortably.

2. Close your eyes and take a few deep breaths to center yourself.

3. Bring to mind a person or situation that you need to forgive.

4. Silently repeat the phrase, "I forgive you, and I release you from my anger and pain."

5. Allow yourself to feel any emotions that arise, and continue this practice until you feel a sense of release.

Self-forgiveness is equally important. Reflect on any guilt or self-blame you may be carrying and practice self-compassion. Remind yourself that everyone makes mistakes and that you deserve forgiveness and healing.

Step 4: Seeking Professional Support

Sometimes, professional support is necessary to navigate deep-seated traumas. A therapist or counselor can provide valuable guidance and tools for healing. Look for a therapist who specializes in trauma and relationship issues. This professional can help you explore your traumas in a safe and structured environment and provide strategies for healing and improving your relationship. Couples therapy can be particularly beneficial for addressing shared traumas and improving communication. A therapist can guide you through difficult conversations and help you develop healthier patterns of interaction.

Practical Exercises to Implement

Healing emotional scars and navigating past traumas is a gradual process that requires dedication and patience. Engaging in activities that promote healing and connection can strengthen your relationship and help you navigate past traumas together. Here are some practical exercises you can implement to facilitate healing and strengthen your relationship.

Exercise 1: Emotional Check-Ins

Regular emotional check-ins can help you stay connected and address any issues before they escalate.

1. Set Aside Time: Choose a regular time each week for your check-in when both partners are relaxed and free from distractions.

2. Create a Safe Space: Ensure that your environment is comfortable and private.

3. Share and Listen: Take turns sharing how you feel, what has been on your mind, and any concerns or needs. Practice active listening and validate each other's feelings.

4. Discuss Solutions: If any issues arise, discuss possible solutions together. Focus on collaboration and mutual support.

Exercise 2: Guided Imagery for Healing

Guided imagery can help you visualize healing and release negative emotions.

1. Find a Quiet Space: Sit or lie down in a quiet space where you won't be disturbed.

2. Relax Your Body: Close your eyes and take several deep breaths to relax your body.

3. Visualize a Safe Place: Imagine a place where you feel completely safe and at peace. This could be a real location or a place you create in your mind.

4. Invite Healing: Visualize a warm, healing light surrounding you. Imagine this light entering your body, healing any emotional wounds and releasing negative emotions.

5. Stay with the Image: Stay with this image for as long as you feel comfortable, allowing yourself to fully experience healing and peace.

Exercise 3: Collaborative Goal Setting

Setting collaborative goals can help you work together towards healing and improving your relationship.

1. Identify Areas for Improvement: Discuss areas of your relationship that you want to improve. These could be related to communication, trust, intimacy, or any other aspect.

2. Set Specific Goals: Set specific, measurable goals you can work towards together. For example, "We will have a weekly date night to strengthen our connection."

3. Create an Action Plan: Develop an action plan outlining the steps you will take to achieve these goals. Assign responsibilities and set timelines.

4. Review and Adjust: Review your progress regularly and adjust your goals as needed. Celebrate your achievements and continue working towards your shared vision.

Exercise 4: Mindfulness and Meditation

Mindfulness and meditation can help you stay present and manage stress and anxiety related to past traumas.

1. Find a Quiet Space: Sit comfortably in a quiet space where you won't be disturbed.

2. Focus on Your Breath: Close your eyes and focus on your breath. Notice the sensation of the air entering and leaving your body.

3. Observe Your Thoughts: Allow your thoughts to come and go without judgment. Simply observe them and return your focus to your breath.

4. Practice Regularly: Practice this mindfulness exercise for a few minutes daily to develop greater awareness and emotional regulation.

Exercise 5: Healing Through Art

Art can be a powerful medium for expressing and processing emotions. Consider engaging in creative activities together, such as painting, drawing, or crafting. These activities provide a safe outlet for expressing feelings that are difficult to articulate in words.

1. Set Up a Creative Space: Designate a space in your home for creative activities. Gather materials such as paints, markers, clay, or any other art supplies you enjoy.

2. Choose a Project: Select a project that feels meaningful to both of you. This could be a collaborative piece or an individual project that you share with each other.

3. Express Emotions: Use the creative process to express your emotions. Allow yourself to explore your feelings through colors, shapes, and forms.

4. Share and Reflect: Share your artwork with each other and reflect on the emotions and experiences it represents. Use this as a starting point for deeper conversations about your healing journey.

Exercise 6: Nature Walks

Spending time in nature can be incredibly therapeutic. Consider taking regular walks together in natural settings like parks, forests, or beaches. The tranquility of nature can provide a calming environment for reflection and connection.

1. Plan Regular Outings: Schedule regular nature walks together and make them a part of your routine. Choose locations that you both enjoy and feel comfortable in.

2. Be Present: During your walks, focus on being present and fully experiencing the sights, sounds, and smells of nature. Use this time to disconnect from daily stressors and reconnect with each other.

3. Reflect and Share: Use your walks as an opportunity to reflect on your healing journey and share your thoughts and feelings with each other. Let nature's serenity guide your conversations and provide a peaceful backdrop for emotional exploration.

Exercise 7: Mindful Touch

Mindful touch can be a powerful way to reconnect physically and emotionally. This involves being fully present and attentive during moments of physical contact, such as holding hands, hugging, or massaging each other.

1. Create a Relaxing Environment: Set up a relaxing environment with dim lighting, soothing music, and comfortable seating or lying arrangements.

2. Be Present: Focus on being fully present during moments of physical contact. Pay attention to the sensations and emotions that arise.

3. Communicate: Communicate your needs and preferences with each other. Use this time to express appreciation and affection through touch.

4. Practice Regularly: Incorporate mindful touch into your daily routine, using it to reconnect and express love and support.

In addition to working together as a couple, building a supportive community can provide additional resources and encouragement. Connecting with others who have experienced similar traumas can provide a sense of solidarity and support. Consider joining a support group or online community where you can share your experiences and learn from others. There are many professional resources available for those dealing with trauma. These include books, online courses, and workshops offering valuable insights and healing strategies. Seek out reputable sources that align with your needs and values, and don't hesitate to ask for help when needed. Surround yourself with supportive friends and family who can offer encouragement and understanding. Share your journey with those you trust, and allow them to provide the emotional support you need. Building a network of people who understand and empathize with your struggles can be incredibly healing.

A Message from the Coles

Healing emotional scars and navigating past traumas is a deeply personal and often challenging journey. Reflecting on this chapter, we are reminded of our experiences and growth together. We want to share some final thoughts and encouragement as you continue your healing journey. Healing takes time, and it's important to be patient with yourself and your partner. There will be moments of progress and moments of difficulty, but remember that each step you take is a step toward healing. Show compassion towards yourself and each other, and celebrate the small victories along the way.

Open communication is essential for healing. Continue to create a safe space for honest conversations and practice active listening. Share your thoughts, feelings, and experiences with each other, and support each other through the ups and downs. Your willingness to communicate openly will strengthen your bond and foster deeper understanding. Don't hesitate to seek professional support when needed. Therapists, counselors, and support groups can provide valuable guidance and resources. There is no shame in seeking help; doing so can be a powerful step towards healing and growth. Stay connected with each other and with your supportive community. Engage in activities that promote healing and connection, and surround yourself with people who understand and support your journey. Remember that you are not alone, and there is strength in connection.

As you navigate the sensitive terrain of healing emotional scars and navigating past traumas, the Passion Pathway Program stands ready to support you. By joining our community, you gain access to additional resources and compassionate support that can make your healing process more manageable and less isolating. Let us accompany you as you work through these challenges together, ensuring a healthier, more resilient relationship.

You are resilient, and you have the strength to heal and grow. Believe in your ability to overcome challenges and build a fulfilling and passionate relationship. Trust in the process, and know you can achieve the love and connection you desire. We are honored to be a part of your journey and are committed to supporting you every step of the way. Healing emotional scars and navigating past traumas is a profound and transformative process, and we believe in your ability to succeed. Embrace the journey with courage and hope, and know we are here with you. Thank you for trusting us with your hearts and your journey. We are excited to see the growth and healing that lies ahead for you and your partner. Together, you can overcome the past and create a future filled with love, trust, and deep connection.

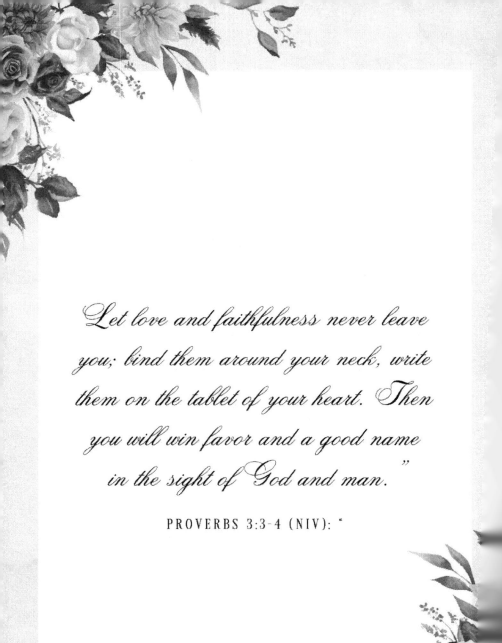

Let love and faithfulness never leave you; bind them around your neck, write them on the tablet of your heart. Then you will win favor and a good name in the sight of God and man."

PROVERBS 3:3-4 (NIV): "

Chapter 4:
DEEPENING CONNECTION: ENHANCING INTIMACY IN YOUR RELATIONSHIP

Welcome to Chapter 4 of our journey towards a more fulfilling and passionate relationship. In this chapter, we will explore the vital aspects of deepening your emotional and physical connection with your partner while enhancing intimacy on multiple levels. We have learned that intimacy extends far beyond the physical; it encompasses emotional, intellectual, and spiritual dimensions that are equally important for a thriving relationship.

Intimacy is about feeling close and connected to your partner, sharing your inner world, and experiencing mutual trust and affection. Our goal in this chapter is to provide practical strategies and exercises to strengthen your bond, increase your understanding of each other, and enhance your overall intimacy. Intimacy is often associated with physical closeness and sexual activity, but it encompasses much more. A truly intimate relationship involves emotional, intellectual, and spiritual connection, creating a deep sense of togetherness and mutual understanding.

Emotional intimacy is sharing your deepest feelings, fears, and desires with your partner. It involves vulnerability, trusting your partner with your innermost thoughts, and feeling supported and understood.

Intellectual intimacy is about sharing ideas, thoughts, and interests. It involves engaging in meaningful conversations, exploring new concepts together, and stimulating each other's minds.

Spiritual intimacy involves sharing your beliefs, values, and experiences related to spirituality. This can include discussing your faith, practicing spiritual activities together, and supporting each other's spiritual growth.

Understanding these different dimensions of intimacy can help you identify areas for strengthening your connection and creating a more holistic bond with your partner.

Enhancing Intimacy on Multiple Levels

Enhancing intimacy in your relationship requires intentional effort and a willingness to explore new ways of connecting. Here are some practical steps to help you deepen your connection on emotional, intellectual, and spiritual levels. Also included are additional steps on non-sexual physical affection, sexual intimacy, creating a supportive and loving environment, and supporting each other's personal and professional growth.

Step 1: Building Emotional Intimacy

Emotional intimacy is the foundation of a deep and lasting connection. It involves sharing your feelings, being vulnerable, and supporting each other through life's ups and downs.

As discussed in previous chapters, creating a safe space is crucial for open and honest communication. Ensure that both partners feel secure in expressing their emotions without fear of judgment or rejection.

Make it a habit to share your feelings with your partner regularly. This can be done through daily check-ins, where you discuss your day and share your thoughts and emotions. Be honest about your feelings and encourage your partner to do the same.

Active listening is essential for building emotional intimacy. When your partner shares their feelings, listen attentively, validate their emotions, and show empathy. Avoid interrupting or offering solutions unless your partner asks for advice.

Exercise: Emotional Journaling and Sharing

1. Journaling: Spend a few minutes journaling about your feelings and experiences each day. Reflect on what made you happy, sad, or stressed, and write down your thoughts.

2. Sharing: At the end of the week, share some of your journal entries with your partner. Discuss your feelings and listen to your partner's reflections as well.

3. Reflection: Reflect on how this exercise helped you better understand each other and strengthened your emotional connection.

Step 2: Enhancing Intellectual Intimacy

Intellectual intimacy involves stimulating each other's minds and sharing ideas and interests. Engaging in intellectual activities together can strengthen your bond and create a deeper connection.

Set aside time for meaningful conversations where you discuss topics of mutual interest. This could include current events, books, movies, or philosophical questions. The goal is to explore each other's thoughts and opinions and learn from each other.

Explore new hobbies or activities that interest both of you. This could include taking a cooking class, learning a new language, or starting a DIY project. Sharing new experiences can enhance your intellectual connection and create lasting memories.

Exercise: Intellectual Date Nights

1. Choose a Topic: Select a topic of mutual interest to explore together. This could be a book, documentary, or article.

2. Discussion: Plan a date night where you discuss the topic in depth. Share your thoughts, ask questions, and listen to each other's perspectives.

3. Reflection: Reflect on how the discussion has enriched your understanding of each other and strengthened your intellectual connection.

Step 3: Deepening Spiritual Intimacy

Spiritual intimacy involves sharing your beliefs, values, and spiritual practices. This connection can provide a sense of purpose and meaning in your relationship.

Discuss your spiritual beliefs and values with your partner. Share your spiritual journey and listen to your partner's experiences. Respect each other's perspectives and support each other's spiritual growth.

Engage in spiritual activities that are meaningful to both of you. This could include praying, meditating, attending religious services, or practicing mindfulness. These activities can create a sense of unity and deepen your spiritual connection.

Exercise: Spiritual Reflection and Sharing

1. Individual Reflection: Spend some time reflecting on your spiritual journey and what spirituality means to you. Write down your thoughts and experiences.

2. Sharing: Share your reflections with your partner and discuss your spiritual beliefs, values, and practices.

3. Joint Activity: Choose a spiritual activity to do together, such as meditating, praying, or attending a religious service.

4. Reflection: Reflect on how this exercise has strengthened your spiritual connection and created a sense of unity.

Step 4: Enhancing Non-Sexual Physical Affection

While physical intimacy often involves sexual activity, it also includes non-sexual touch and affection, which are crucial for a healthy relationship.

Non-sexual physical affection, such as holding hands, hugging, and cuddling, can enhance your emotional connection and create a sense of closeness.

Make physical affection a regular part of your routine. This could include starting and ending your day with a hug or kiss, holding hands while walking, or cuddling while watching a movie.

Exercise: The 20-Second Hug

1. Commit: Commit to giving each other a 20-second hug daily. This simple act can release oxytocin, a hormone that promotes bonding and reduces stress.

2. Embrace: Stand facing each other and embrace for a full 20 seconds. Focus on the physical sensations and the emotional connection.

3. Reflect: Reflect on how this daily practice has strengthened your bond and enhanced your sense of closeness.

Step 5: Enhancing Sexual Intimacy

Sexual intimacy is an important aspect of a healthy relationship. It's about physical pleasure, emotional connection, and mutual satisfaction.

Discuss your sexual needs, desires, and boundaries openly and honestly. Ensure that both partners feel comfortable expressing their preferences and concerns.

Be open to exploring new ways to connect sexually. This could include trying new activities and positions or incorporating sensual activities such as massages or baths.

Exercise: Sensual Exploration Date

1. Plan a Date: Plan a date dedicated to exploring each other's sensual preferences. This could include giving each other massages, bathing together, or exploring different types of touch.

2. Communicate: Openly communicate what feels good and what you want to try. Focus on creating a relaxed and enjoyable experience.

3. Reflect: Reflect on how this experience has enhanced your sexual intimacy and brought you closer together.

Step 6: Creating a Supportive and Loving Environment

Creating a supportive and loving environment is crucial for deepening your connection and enhancing intimacy. This involves fostering mutual respect, appreciation, and support.

Regularly show appreciation for your partner and acknowledge their efforts. This can strengthen your bond and create a positive and supportive atmosphere.

Exercise: Gratitude Journal

1. Journaling: Write down three things you appreciate about your partner daily. These can be small acts of kindness, qualities you admire, or moments that made you feel loved.

2. Sharing: At the end of the week, share your gratitude journal with your partner. Discuss how these moments have made you feel and how you can continue to show appreciation for each other.

3. Reflection: Reflect on how this practice has enhanced your sense of appreciation and strengthened your relationship.

Step 7: Support Each Other's Personal and Professional Growth

Support each other's personal and professional growth. Encourage your partner's goals and dreams and support them to achieve them.

Exercise: Goal Setting and Support

1. Discuss Goals: Discuss your individual goals and dreams with each other. Share what you'd like to achieve and what support you need.

2. Set Joint Goals: Set joint goals that you can work towards together. This could include relationship goals, financial goals, or health goals.

3. Provide Support: Regularly check in with each other and provide the support needed to achieve these goals. Celebrate each other's successes and offer encouragement during challenges.

4. Reflection: Reflect on how supporting each other's growth has strengthened your bond and enhanced your sense of partnership.

Deepening your connection and enhancing intimacy requires intentional effort and a commitment to exploring new ways to connect.

Focusing on emotional, intellectual, spiritual, and physical intimacy can create a more fulfilling and passionate relationship. This includes focusing on non-sexual physical affection, sexual intimacy, creating a supportive and loving environment, and supporting each other's personal and professional growth.

A Message from the Coles

As we reflect on this chapter, we are reminded of the importance of intimacy in our own relationship. We've learned that intimacy is about physical closeness and creating a deep and meaningful connection on multiple levels. We want to share some final thoughts and encouragement as you continue your journey to deepen your connection and enhance intimacy.

Intimacy requires vulnerability. It's about opening up and sharing your true self with your partner, even when it's difficult. Embrace vulnerability as a strength and an opportunity to grow closer. Trust that your partner will respect and cherish you.

Make your relationship a priority. In the hustle and bustle of daily life, it's easy to let intimacy take a backseat. Be intentional about spending quality time together, engaging in meaningful conversations, and nurturing your connection. Prioritizing your relationship will pay off in deeper intimacy and a stronger bond.

Intimacy is built in the small, everyday moments. Celebrate these moments and recognize their importance. Whether it's a shared laugh, a comforting hug, or a quiet evening together, these moments create the foundation of your relationship. Cherish them and let them strengthen your bond. Stay curious about your partner. Even if you've been together for years, there's always more to learn about each other. Ask questions, explore new interests, and continue to grow together. This curiosity keeps your relationship dynamic and deepens your connection.

Find joy in your journey together. Intimacy should be a source of happiness and fulfillment. Seek out activities that bring you both joy and laughter. Share new experiences, create beautiful memories, and let joy be a guiding force in your relationship.

In this chapter, you've explored ways to deepen your connection and enhance intimacy. To continue building on these valuable insights, consider joining the Passion Pathway Program, where you can explore further with others who are on the same path. Our community provides a safe space to share experiences, learn from each other, and continue to grow in intimacy and connection. We are honored to be a part of your journey and are committed to supporting you every step of the way. Deepening your connection and enhancing intimacy is a profound and transformative process, and we believe in your ability to succeed. Embrace the journey with love and hope, and know that we are here with you.

Thank you for trusting us with your hearts and your journey. We are excited to see the growth and deepening connection that lies ahead for you and your partner. Together, you can create a relationship filled with love, trust, and profound intimacy. As you continue this journey, remember that deepening your connection and enhancing intimacy is a continuous process. Each step brings you closer to a stronger, more resilient relationship. Embrace the challenges, celebrate the victories, and continue to support each other with love and compassion. Here's to deepening your connection and creating a future filled with passion and profound intimacy. We believe in you and are excited to see where this journey takes you.

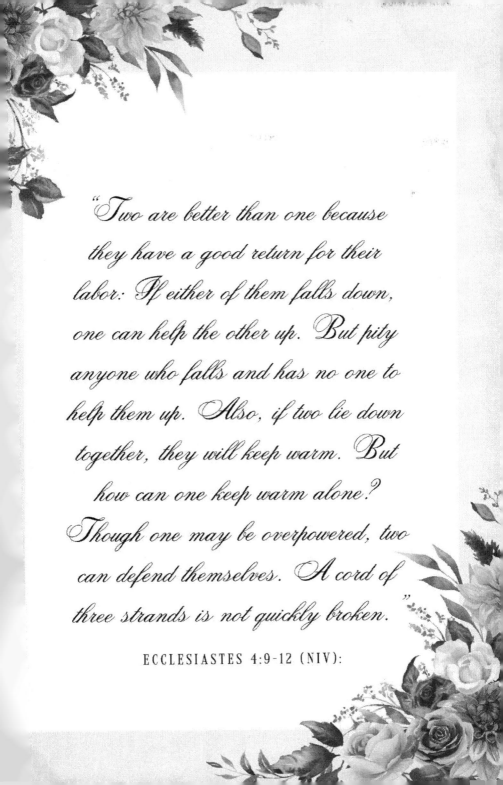

"Two are better than one because they have a good return for their labor: If either of them falls down, one can help the other up. But pity anyone who falls and has no one to help them up. Also, if two lie down together, they will keep warm. But how can one keep warm alone? Though one may be overpowered, two can defend themselves. A cord of three strands is not quickly broken."

ECCLESIASTES 4:9-12 (NIV):

Chapter 5:
EMBRACING SENSUALITY: CULTIVATING PLEASURE IN YOUR RELATIONSHIP

*W*elcome to Chapter 5 of our journey together. This chapter is all about embracing sensuality and cultivating pleasure in your relationship. By focusing on the sensory aspects of intimacy, you can deepen your connection and enhance your sexual fulfillment. In this chapter, we will explore the role of pleasure in sexual fulfillment and provide actionable steps to help you and your partner embrace sensuality in your relationship.

Pleasure is a fundamental aspect of sexual fulfillment. It encompasses physical sensations, emotional connections, and the joy of shared experiences. Understanding and embracing pleasure can enhance your relationship's overall satisfaction and intimacy. Pleasure is a physical sensation and a holistic experience involving your mind, body, and emotions. It creates a sense of well-being, reduces stress, and strengthens the bond between partners. You can improve your overall quality of life and relationship satisfaction by prioritizing pleasure. Many people have misconceptions about pleasure and its role in sexual fulfillment. Some may view it as selfish or indulgent, while others may feel uncomfortable exploring their desires. Addressing these misconceptions and recognizing that pleasure is a natural and healthy part of a loving relationship is essential.

Exploring Sensory Awareness and Sensual Exploration

It is important to explore sensory awareness and engage in sensual exploration to cultivate pleasure. Focusing on your senses and being present in the moment can enhance your connection and deepen your intimacy.

Sensory Awareness: Shared Sensual Experiences

Sensory awareness involves paying attention to the sights, sounds, smells, tastes, and textures around you. By being mindful of your senses, you can fully experience and appreciate the present moment.

This mindfulness in shared sensual experiences can enhance intimacy and create a deeper connection with your partner. Engaging in activities that focus on pleasure and sensory awareness creates lasting memories and strengthens your bond.

Creating shared sensual experiences to cultivate a deeper connection and enhance intimacy is essential. One effective way to do this is by planning regular sensual dates. These dates provide dedicated time for you and your partner to focus on each other and explore new activities together, helping to keep the romance alive and strengthen your connection.

In addition to planning dates, establish sensory rituals you can enjoy together. This could include a nightly massage, a weekly bath, or a morning cuddle session. These rituals help create a sense of intimacy and connection, making your everyday interactions more meaningful.

Exploring new environments is another excellent way to enhance your relationship. Visit a new restaurant, take a trip to a spa, or go on a nature hike. Experiencing new places and activities together can create shared memories and deepen your bond, adding excitement and variety to your relationship.

During your shared sensual experiences, focus on being present and mindful. Pay attention to your senses and the sensations you are experiencing. This mindfulness can enhance your connection and increase pleasure, allowing you to appreciate and enjoy the moment with your partner fully.

Lastly, communicate openly and reflect on your experiences. Throughout your shared sensual experiences, discuss what you enjoy and what feels good. Afterward, take some time to reflect together on the experience and discuss any new insights or discoveries. This open communication and reflection help ensure that both partners are satisfied and can continue to grow and improve their sexual connection.

Sensual Exploration: Pleasure Mapping Exercise

Sensual exploration is about discovering new ways to experience pleasure and intimacy. It involves experimenting with different activities, techniques, and environments to find what brings you and your partner the most joy and satisfaction.

One effective way to explore pleasure is through a pleasure mapping exercise. This activity helps you identify and communicate your desires, preferences, and boundaries, creating a deeper understanding of each other's needs.

First, set the mood by creating a comfortable and relaxing environment to begin your pleasure mapping journey. Light candles, play soft music, and ensure you won't be interrupted. This sets the stage for a calm and intimate exploration. Before you begin this activity, discussing your boundaries or limitations is essential. This conversation ensures that you both feel safe and respected during the exercise, fostering trust and openness.

Next, explore individually by taking turns to explore different areas of your body. Note what feels pleasurable by using a variety of touches, pressures, and techniques. This self-exploration helps you discover what you enjoy and provides valuable insights into your preferences.

After your individual exploration, communicate your findings with your partner. Discuss what felt good, what didn't, and any new insights you gained about your desires and preferences. Open communication enhances mutual understanding and intimacy.

Finally, practice together by using the information you've gathered to enhance your intimate experiences. Incorporate new techniques and touches into your lovemaking to increase pleasure and satisfaction. This shared knowledge can deepen your connection and make your sexual experiences more fulfilling.

Reminders: When Planning Your Sensual Awareness and Exploration Dates

Sensual awareness and exploration dates are a fun and engaging way to deepen your connection and enhance pleasure. These dates focus on sensory activities that heighten awareness and create a memorable and enjoyable experience.

1. **Choose Your Activities**: Select activities that engage your senses and promote intimacy. Some ideas include:
   - **Cooking Together**: Prepare a meal together, focusing on the tastes, smells, and textures of the ingredients.
   - **Massage**: Give each other a relaxing massage, using different oils and techniques to explore what feels best.
   - **Bathing**: Take a bath or shower together, using scented soaps and gentle touches to create a soothing and sensual experience.

o **Nature Walk**: Go for a walk in nature, paying attention to the sights, sounds, and smells around you. Hold hands, hug, and kiss along the way.

2. **Be Present in the Moment**: During your sensual exploration date, focus on being present and fully engaged with your partner. Pay attention to your senses and enjoy the experience without distractions.

3. **Communicate**: Throughout your date, communicate openly with your partner about what feels good and what you enjoy. This helps to create a deeper understanding of each other's desires and preferences.

4. **Reflect**: After your date, take some time to reflect on the experience together. Discuss what you enjoyed, any new insights you gained, and how you can incorporate more sensual exploration into your relationship.

Embracing Pleasure Preferences

Understanding and embracing each other's pleasure preferences is key to cultivating a fulfilling and satisfying sexual relationship. Acknowledging and respecting your partner's desires can create a more intimate and enjoyable connection. To fully embrace and enhance your sexual relationship, it is crucial to discuss your pleasure preferences openly and honestly. Start by having a candid conversation with your partner about what you enjoy, what turns you on, and any fantasies or desires you have. This openness creates a foundation for mutual understanding and deeper connection.

Respecting each other's boundaries is equally important. Creating a safe and trusting environment ensures both partners feel comfortable expressing their desires. Acknowledging and respecting limitations helps foster a sense of security and intimacy.

Experimenting together is another key step. Try new activities, techniques, and experiences to discover what brings you both pleasure. Be open to exploring new things and learning from each other, which can lead to exciting and fulfilling sexual experiences.

Providing feedback during and after intimate experiences is essential for growth. Share your thoughts and feelings with your partner to ensure that both of you are satisfied and can continue to improve your sexual connection. Constructive feedback helps refine and enhance your intimate moments.

Lastly, celebrate the differences in your pleasure preferences. Embrace the unique desires each partner brings to the relationship. Understanding and appreciating these differences can help create a more inclusive and satisfying sexual relationship, enriching your bond and deepening your connection.

A Message from the Coles

As we conclude this chapter on embracing sensuality and cultivating pleasure, we want to leave you with a heartfelt message. This journey of exploring pleasure and deepening your connection is beautiful and transformative. Embrace the journey of exploring pleasure and sensuality with an open heart and a willingness to learn and grow. Remember that this journey is unique to you and your partner, and it is a beautiful opportunity to deepen your bond and enhance your relationship. Take time to celebrate each other and the progress you have made together. Recognize the effort and dedication you have both invested in your relationship and celebrate the joy and pleasure you have discovered together.

Stay committed to each other and to the journey of exploring pleasure and sensuality. There will be challenges along the way, but with commitment, love, and understanding, you can overcome them together and continue to grow and thrive. Keep exploring new ways to experience pleasure and deepen your connection. Be open to trying new things, learning from each other, and continually seeking ways to enhance your relationship.

We are deeply grateful for the opportunity to share this journey with you. Your trust and openness have been a gift, and we are honored to have been a part of your growth. We believe in your ability to create a fulfilling and passionate relationship, and we are excited to see where this journey takes you. Having delved into the joy of embracing pleasure and cultivating sensuality, why not extend this delightful exploration? Joining the Passion Pathway Program can enhance your experience, providing structured guidance and a supportive community that cheers on your every discovery. Together, let's continue to explore the art of pleasure in ways that continually renew and enrich your relationship. Thank you for allowing us to be a part of your story. We wish you all the love, joy, and connection as you continue building a beautiful life together.

With love and gratitude,

The Coles

"Above all, love each other deeply, because love covers over a multitude of sins."

1 PETER 4:8 (NIV)

Chapter 6:

INTEGRATING GROWTH: MASTERING YOUR JOURNEY TO LASTING SEXUAL FULFILLMENT

*W*elcome to the final chapter of our journey together. This chapter will reflect on your progress and celebrate your achievements. We'll also discuss how to integrate the growth you've experienced and create a sustainable plan for lasting sexual fulfillment. By the end of this chapter, you'll have concrete strategies to maintain the intimacy, pleasure, and connection you've cultivated over the past weeks.

Reflecting on your journey is crucial in understanding how far you've come and what you've achieved. It helps to solidify the changes you've made and prepares you for continued growth. Reflection allows you to see the progress you've made and the challenges you've overcome. It's an opportunity to acknowledge the hard work and dedication you've both invested in improving your relationship.

Celebrating milestones is an important part of this process. Identify key moments in your journey where you experienced communication, intimacy, or emotional healing breakthroughs. Celebrate these milestones together, recognizing the effort and commitment each of you has shown.

Take time to acknowledge the growth you've experienced individually and as a couple. Reflect on how you've changed and improved and how these changes have positively impacted your relationship.

Sharing your gratitude for each other and your journey together is equally important. Expressing gratitude strengthens your bond and fosters a positive outlook for the future.

Reflecting on your progress helps to consolidate your achievements and identify areas for continued growth. While reflecting, list your achievements and be specific about the changes you've seen in your relationship and how they've impacted your connection. Also, acknowledge any challenges you've faced, consider how you overcame them, and what you learned from them.

In addition, anticipate potential challenges that could arise and develop strategies to address them. Having a plan in place can help you navigate difficulties more effectively. Create a sustainability plan to ensure continued growth and connection in your relationship. As part of your sustainability plan, start with a progress reflection exercise.

Progress Reflection Exercise

Take some time to sit down together and reflect on the past weeks. Use the following prompts to guide your reflection:

1. What were the most significant moments for you during this journey?
2. How has your relationship changed since you began this program?
3. What have you learned about yourself and your partner?
4. What are you most proud of in your journey?
5. How do you feel about the future of your relationship?

Creating a plan to sustain the growth and connection you've cultivated is essential as you look to the future. This plan will help you maintain your progress and continue building a strong, fulfilling relationship.

Your sustainability plan should include regular check-ins, date nights, continued learning, goal setting, and building a support network.

Regular Check-Ins

Regular check-ins are vital. Schedule regular check-ins to discuss your relationship. These check-ins can help you stay connected, address any issues that arise, and celebrate ongoing growth. Regular discussions about the relationship can lead to positive changes and improvements. They help couples continuously grow and adapt to each other's needs and expectations. Consider setting aside time weekly or monthly for these conversations.

Date Nights

Prioritizing regular date nights will help keep the romance alive. Use these nights as dedicated time to explore new activities, revisit favorite experiences, and focus on each other. Regular date nights help reinforce your emotional bond and intimacy. Life can get busy with work, family, and other responsibilities. Date nights offer a chance to reconnect and enjoy each other's company without distractions. Date nights help maintain the romantic aspect of the relationship, ensuring that the partnership doesn't become purely functional or routine.

Continued Learning

Commit to continued learning and exploration. As individuals grow and change, so do their needs and desires. Continuous learning and exploration help couples adapt to these changes and stay connected. Read books, attend workshops, or take courses together to keep your relationship dynamic and evolving. Learning new things together can spark conversations and deepen understanding. It encourages open dialogue about each partner's thoughts and feelings, enhancing overall communication.

Goal Setting

Based on your reflection, set goals for the future. These goals should be specific, measurable, achievable, relevant, and time-bound (SMART). Setting goals is a key component of your relationship. Regularly reviewing and adjusting them as needed is also essential. These goals relate to communication, intimacy, personal growth, or shared activities. Having clear goals provides motivation and purpose. It helps both partners stay focused and committed to making positive changes and improvements in their relationship and life together. Working towards and achieving goals together can create a sense of accomplishment and fulfillment, reinforcing the satisfaction and enjoyment in the relationship.

Build a Support Network

Building a support network of friends, mentors, or professionals who can offer guidance and encouragement is equally important. Having a community to lean on can provide valuable support during challenging times. A supportive community can also encourage couples to pursue their goals and dreams, offering motivation and reinforcement during times of uncertainty or self-doubt. Observing and interacting with other healthy relationships within the support network can provide positive examples and reinforce effective relationship practices.

Summary

Having concrete strategies as a sustainability plan to maintain the intimacy, pleasure, and connection you've cultivated over the past weeks is essential. Reflecting on your journey is crucial in understanding how far you've come and what you've achieved. Discuss your achievements, challenges, and goals for the future. Identify your top priorities for sustaining your relationship's growth. These include regular check-ins, date nights, continued learning, goal setting, and building a support network. Then, create a schedule for your top priorities and other activities that support your relationship. Ensure that both partners are committed to following this schedule. Identify the support systems you'll rely on, such as friends, mentors, or professionals, and discuss how these systems can provide guidance and encouragement. Plan to review and adjust your sustainability plan as needed regularly. Relationships are dynamic, and it's important to remain flexible and open to change.

Commitment Prayer

As you conclude your sustainability planning session, consider incorporating a commitment prayer to reaffirm your dedication to each other and your journey. This prayer can be a powerful way to seal your commitment to ongoing growth and connection.

Commitment Prayer Example:

"Dear God,

We come before you with grateful hearts, thankful for the journey we've undertaken together. We acknowledge the growth we've experienced and the love we've cultivated. We commit to continuing this journey with open hearts and minds, dedicated to supporting each other through every challenge and celebrating every triumph. We ask for your guidance and strength as we strive to maintain the intimacy, pleasure, and connection we've built. Bless our relationship and help us to always communicate with love, compassion, and understanding. May we continue to grow together, deepening our bond and nurturing our love for each other.

Amen."

A Message from the Coles

As we conclude this final chapter, we want to leave you with a heartfelt message from us. This journey has been deeply personal and transformative for us, and we hope it has also been for you. Your journey toward lasting sexual fulfillment is unique and personal. Embrace it with an open heart and a willingness to grow and learn. Remember that every step you take brings you closer to a stronger, more connected relationship. Take time to celebrate your achievements, both big and small. Recognize the progress you've made and the effort you've invested. Celebrating your successes reinforces positive behaviors and encourages continued growth. Stay committed to each other and your relationship. There will be challenges along the way, but with commitment, love, and determination, you can overcome them together. Trust in your ability to navigate the ups and downs of life as a team. Relationships are dynamic and ever-evolving. Keep learning about each other, exploring new ideas, and seeking ways to deepen your connection. This continuous learning keeps your relationship vibrant and exciting.

As you conclude this initial journey and look forward to a future of sustained growth and sexual fulfillment, remember that the road does not end here. By joining the Passion Pathway Program, you ensure ongoing support and guidance as you implement what you've learned and continue to evolve together. Let us help you keep the momentum going with resources, support, and a community that understands and shares your commitment to a fulfilling relationship.

We are incredibly grateful for the opportunity to share this journey with you. Your trust and openness have been a gift, and we are honored to have been a part of your growth. We believe in your ability to create a fulfilling and passionate relationship, and we are excited to see where this journey takes you. Thank you for allowing us to be a part of your story. We wish you all the love, joy, and connection as you continue building a beautiful life together.

With love and gratitude,

The Coles

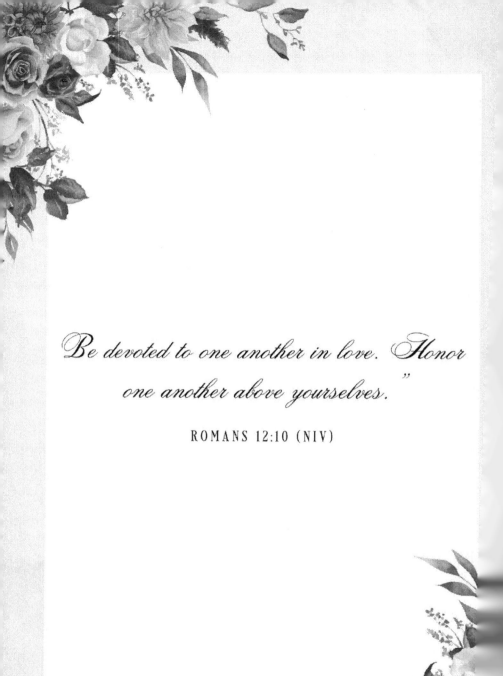

Be devoted to one another in love. Honor one another above yourselves. "

ROMANS 12:10 (NIV)

Conclusion

As we come to the end of this journey, it's important to take a moment to celebrate the progress you've made and look forward to the future. Throughout this program, you have embarked on a transformative journey toward a more fulfilling and passionate relationship. Each step has been vital to this journey, from establishing a strong foundation and mastering communication to healing emotional scars and deepening intimacy. You've learned to embrace pleasure and integrate these lessons into your daily lives, setting the stage for lasting sexual fulfillment.

Reflect on how far you've come since you began this program. Think about the insights you've gained, the new skills you've developed, and the deepened connection you now share with your partner. Celebrate the small victories and the significant milestones, for each one represents a step closer to a more intimate, loving, and fulfilling relationship.

We, the Coles, want to leave you with some final words of encouragement. Remember that the journey to sexual fulfillment and deep connection is ongoing. There will be challenges along the way, but with faith, communication, and a commitment to each other, you can overcome any obstacle. Keep nurturing your relationship, keep exploring each other's desires, and never stop learning and growing together. You have the tools and the foundation now; continue to build on them with love, patience, and dedication. As you continue to nurture your relationship and deepen your connection, may these scriptures offer you guidance, strength, and inspiration:

1. **1 Corinthians 13:4-7 (NIV):** "Love is patient, love is kind. It does not envy, it does not boast, it is not proud. It does not dishonor others; it is not self-seeking; it is not easily angered; it keeps no record of wrongs. Love does not delight in evil but rejoices with the truth. It always protects, always trusts, always hopes, always perseveres."

2. **Ephesians 4:2-3 (NIV)** "Be completely humble and gentle; be patient, bearing with one another in love. Make every effort to keep the unity of the Spirit through the bond of peace."

3. **Colossians 3:14 (NIV)** "And over all these virtues put on love, which binds them all together in perfect unity."

4. **Proverbs 3:3-4 (NIV):** "Let love and faithfulness never leave you; bind them around your neck, write them on the tablet of your heart. Then you will win favor and a good name in the sight of God and man."

5. **Ecclesiastes 4:9-12 (NIV):** "Two are better than one because they have a good return for their labor: If either of them falls down, one can help the other up. But pity anyone who falls and has no one to help them up. Also, if two lie down together, they will keep warm. But how can one keep warm alone? Though one may be overpowered, two can defend themselves. A cord of three strands is not quickly broken."

6. **1 Peter 4:8 (NIV):** "Above all, love each other deeply, because love covers over a multitude of sins."

7. **Romans 12:10 (NIV)** "Be devoted to one another in love. Honor one another above yourselves."

8. **Song of Solomon 8:7 (NIV):** "Many waters cannot quench love; rivers cannot sweep it away. If one were to give all the wealth of one's house for love, it would be utterly scorned."

9. **1 John 4:18 (NIV):** "There is no fear in love. But perfect love drives out fear, because fear has to do with punishment. The one who fears is not made perfect in love."

10. **Genesis 2:24 (NIV):** "That is why a man leaves his father and mother and is united to his wife, and they become one flesh."

For those seeking continued growth and support, there are numerous resources available to help you on your journey. Consider reading books on sexual intimacy and relationship building, attending workshops or seminars, and seeking professional counseling if needed. There are also online courses and forums to connect with other couples on similar journeys.

The key is to stay committed to growth and seek the support and resources to help you continue to thrive. We also want to extend an invitation to join the Passion Pathway Community. This community is designed to provide ongoing support and connection for couples who are dedicated to enhancing their relationships. By joining, you'll have access to exclusive resources, regular updates, and a network of like-minded couples who can offer encouragement, advice, and friendship. Together, we can continue to support each other on this journey toward lasting sexual fulfillment and deep connection.

As you move forward, carry with you the lessons you've learned and the progress you've made. Remember that every relationship is unique, and the journey to intimacy is a personal one. Stay open, stay committed, and most importantly, stay connected with each other. Your relationship is a beautiful journey, and we are honored to have been a part of it. Here's to a future filled with passion, love, and profound connection.

With love and blessings,

The Coles

We have created 365 affirming, loving, and supportive quotes for spouses, one for each day of the year. These can help foster love, encouragement, and connection in your marriage. Feel free to hand write these on cards or sticky notes. Get creative, and make it special and fun!

1-31: LOVE & APPRECIATION

1. "You are my heart's greatest treasure, and I am endlessly grateful for you."
2. "Every day with you is a gift I never want to take for granted."
3. "You make my life brighter just by being in it."
4. "I love you more with each passing moment."
5. "I appreciate everything you do, big and small."
6. "I'm thankful for the way you love me."
7. "Your presence in my life is a constant reminder of God's goodness."
8. "You are my favorite person to do life with."
9. "I am so proud to call you mine."
10. "Your love completes me in ways I never knew were possible."
11. "I feel so blessed to walk through life with you by my side."
12. "You bring joy and laughter to my world."
13. "You are my constant source of strength."
14. "I am forever grateful for your love and partnership."
15. "I love the way you make me feel safe and cherished."
16. "Thank you for being my partner, my love, and my best friend."
17. "You are the answer to my prayers."
18. "I love you just as you are, perfectly imperfect."

19. "I am in awe of the love we share."

20. "Being with you makes everything feel right."

21. "You are my home, my heart, my forever."

22. "I am grateful for every moment we spend together."

23. "Loving you is my favorite adventure."

24. "You have the most beautiful soul."

25. "Your smile brightens my darkest days."

26. "I feel so lucky to be loved by you."

27. "I treasure every laugh, every hug, every kiss."

28. "You are the best part of my life."

29. "Thank you for filling my heart with so much love."

30. "You are my heart's greatest joy."

31. "With you, I have everything I need."

32–60: ENCOURAGEMENT & SUPPORT

32. "I believe in you more than anyone else."

33. "You are stronger than you know, and I'll always be here to remind you."

34. "No matter what happens, I'll always have your back."

35. "You inspire me with your strength and resilience."

36. "I love you for who you are, not for what you achieve."

37. "We can conquer anything together."

38. "When you feel like giving up, know that I'm here to hold you up."

39. "I see your potential and believe in everything you do."

40. "You're not alone. I'm right here with you."

41. "Whatever you need, I am here to support you."

42. "I admire your courage and determination."

43. "Your dreams are my dreams, and I'll support them always."

44. "I love your perseverance and commitment to what matters to you."

45. "You are so capable, and I'm proud of everything you accomplish."

46. "I'll always be your biggest cheerleader."

47. "When you fall, I'll be here to lift you up."

48. "Your strength amazes me every single day."

49. "You make me believe that anything is possible."

50. "Together, we can face anything life throws our way."

51. "I love watching you grow and thrive."

52. "I'm so proud of how far you've come."

53. "You don't have to be perfect; I love you just as you are."

54. "I'm here to listen whenever you need to talk."

55. "You're not in this alone; we're in it together."

56. "I believe in your ability to succeed."

57. "I love your heart, your mind, and your spirit."

58. "You have a way of making hard things seem possible."

59. "Whatever life brings, we'll handle it together."

60. "I'll always be your safe place to land."

61-90: EXPRESSIONS OF LOVE

61. "You are my heart's forever love."

62. "I love the way you love me."

63. "I never want to stop holding your hand."

64. "You are my greatest adventure."

65. "I will love you more tomorrow than I do today."

66. "You are the love of my life."

67. "I cherish every moment spent with you."

68. "My love for you knows no bounds."

69. "You make every day more beautiful."

70. "Loving you is the easiest thing I've ever done."

71. "You are my greatest gift."

72. "I love you beyond the stars and back."

73. "I choose you every single day."

74. "You are my forever and always."

75. "I love the way we grow together."

76. "You are the best part of my life."

77. "I am happiest when I am with you."

78. "Every part of me loves every part of you."

79. "You are my heart's home."

80. "I love how safe and loved I feel in your arms."

81. "You make my life infinitely better."

82. "I am so grateful to walk through life with you."

83. "I love how deeply we understand each other."

84. "I am proud to love you."

85. "I love you more than words could ever express."

86. "You are my heart's greatest joy."

87. "Every day, I fall more in love with you."

88. "I love how we support and grow with each other."

89. "You make my world so much brighter."

90. "I love you with every fiber of my being."

91–120: GRATITUDE FOR THE RELATIONSHIP

91. "I'm so thankful for all the ways you show your love."

92. "I am grateful for our journey together."

93. "You have made my life richer and more beautiful."

94. "Thank you for always being there for me."

95. "I appreciate all the little things you do to make me feel loved."

96. "I am so thankful for the love we share."

97. "You are the answer to so many of my prayers."

98. "I feel so blessed to have you in my life."

99. "Thank you for being my person."

100. "You are the reason for so much of my happiness."

101. "I'm grateful for every day we get to spend together."

102. "Thank you for always being my rock."

103. "I feel lucky to wake up beside you every morning."

104. "I am forever grateful for your love and care."

105. "You've made my life better in every way."

106. "Thank you for being my safe haven."

107. "I am grateful for your patience, love, and kindness."

108. "You are my biggest blessing."

109. "I appreciate how much you care for our relationship."

110. "Thank you for being the best partner I could ever ask for."

111. "I am so thankful for the life we've built together."

112. "Your love is a constant reminder of how blessed I am."

113. "You bring out the best in me."

114. "Thank you for choosing to love me every day."

115. "You are the person I've always dreamed of loving."

116. "I feel so blessed to be loved by someone as wonderful as you."

117. "Thank you for all the joy you bring into my life."

118. "I am grateful for our shared moments, both big and small."

119. "Thank you for making me feel valued and cherished."

120. "I appreciate how much you pour into our relationship."

121-365: DEEPER AFFIRMATIONS AND LOVING MESSAGES

121. "I love how safe and cherished I feel when I'm with you."

122. "You are my best friend and greatest love."

123. "I love how we can laugh, cry, and grow together."

124. "You bring so much light into my life."

125. "I love building our future together."

126. "You make me a better person every day."

127. "I love the life we've created and the love we share."

128. "With you, I feel fully seen and deeply loved."

129. "I love that we grow together through every season of life."

130. "Thank you for loving me even when I'm at my worst."

131. "Your love gives me strength and courage."

132. "I appreciate your support and encouragement in all that I do."

133. "I love how we navigate life's ups and downs hand in hand."

134. "You are the love I never knew I needed."

135. "I am so thankful for your gentle heart and loving spirit."

136. "Our love story is my favorite."

137. "Every day with you is a blessing I cherish."

138. "I love the way you make me feel seen and understood."

139. "You are my greatest comfort and joy."

140. "Thank you for your patience, kindness, and love."

141. "You complete me in ways I never thought possible."

142. "I love growing old with you."

143. "You are my greatest source of strength."

144. "I appreciate your unwavering support."

145. "Your love is my safe place."

146. "I love how we communicate and work through challenges."

147. "Thank you for being my rock, my partner, and my love."

148. "I love our shared moments of laughter and joy."

149. "I appreciate your love and understanding."

150. "I am so grateful for your love and care."

151. "You make my heart overflow with love."

152. "I love that we build each other up."

153. "You are the reason my heart feels full."

154. "I appreciate your dedication to our relationship."

155. "You make me feel valued and appreciated."

156. "I love the way we support each other's dreams."

157. "You are my heart's greatest joy."

158. "I appreciate your commitment to us."

159. "I am thankful for the way you love and care for me."

160. "You are my greatest love, my partner, my everything."

161. "I love how we bring out the best in each other."

162. "I love growing with you through every season of life."

163. "Your love is a constant source of happiness."

164. "I am grateful for the joy and laughter we share."

165. "You make life's challenges easier with your love and support."

166. "I am thankful for every moment with you."

167. "Your love makes my world brighter."

168. "I appreciate how we communicate and support one another."

169. "You are my safe place and my greatest love."

170. "Thank you for your unconditional love and care."

171. "I love how we've grown together and continue to build our love."

172. "Your love makes my heart feel safe and cherished."

173. "I am so grateful for your unwavering love and support."

174. "You are my greatest blessing, and I cherish you every day."

175. "I love how our love grows deeper with each passing year."

176. "You inspire me to be the best version of myself."

177. "I am thankful for your love, your strength, and your kindness."

178. "Our love story is my favorite, and I'm so glad it's ours."

179. "You make every day feel special just by being in it."

180. "I feel so lucky to have you as my partner in life and love."

181. "Thank you for making me feel safe, cherished, and adored."

182. "I love the way you make me feel like I'm the only one in the world."

183. "You are my heart's deepest desire, and I'll love you forever."

184. "I cherish the way we laugh, love, and grow together."

185. "You are the person I want to spend the rest of my life with."

186. "I am so grateful for all the love and joy you bring into my life."

187. "Your love is the most precious gift I've ever received."

188. "Thank you for being my partner in every way."

189. "You are my soulmate, and I am thankful every day for you."

190. "I love the way you understand me without needing words."

191. "You make me feel so loved and supported in everything I do."

192. "You are the love I prayed for, and I am so blessed to have you."

193. "I feel so fortunate to share my life with you."

194. "Your love fills my heart with peace and happiness."

195. "I am proud to stand beside you, through all of life's moments."

196. "You are my greatest confidant, my best friend, and my love."

197. "Your love gives me courage when I need it the most."

198. "I feel so loved and cherished by you, and I am forever grateful."

199. "You make even the ordinary moments feel extraordinary."

200. "I am thankful for your love that fills every corner of my heart."

201. "I love how we build each other up and face life's challenges together."

202. "You are my favorite part of every day."

203. "Your love is my constant, and I will treasure it forever."

204. "I feel so blessed to have a partner who loves me the way you do."

205. "You are my biggest supporter, and I love you for it."

206. "Thank you for always being there, for loving me through everything."

207. "You have the most beautiful heart, and I'm so lucky to share mine with you."

208. "You are my forever love, and I wouldn't want it any other way."

209. "Your love fills me with a sense of peace and contentment."

210. "Thank you for being the person I can always count on."

211. "I love the way we communicate and work through life together."

212. "Your love is my constant, and I am forever thankful for it."

213. "I feel so lucky to have found someone as wonderful as you."

214. "You make my world a brighter and more beautiful place."

215. "I love how we've grown together, and I can't wait to see what the future holds."

216. "You are the person who understands me better than anyone."

217. "Your love is a blessing I will never take for granted."

218. "I cherish the moments we share and the memories we make."

219. "You are my heart's greatest joy, and I will love you always."

220. "Thank you for making me feel cherished and loved every day."

221. "Your love fills me with happiness and gratitude."

222. "I appreciate all the little things you do to show you care."

223. "You are my heart's greatest treasure, and I will always love you."

224. "I love the way you love me, and I love you more for it."

225. "You are the most important person in my life, and I cherish you deeply."

226. "I am so thankful for your love, your kindness, and your patience."

227. "You are my rock, my love, and my partner in everything."

228. "I feel so blessed to share my life with someone as wonderful as you."

229. "Your love makes me feel strong, capable, and deeply cherished."

230. "I love the way we laugh together and make the most of every moment."

231. "You are the love of my life, and I will always be grateful for you."

232. "I feel so lucky to have you as my partner, my love, and my best friend."

233. "Your love is a constant reminder of how blessed I am."

234. "I appreciate the way you love and support me in everything I do."

235. "You are my heart's deepest joy, and I will always love you."

236. "Thank you for loving me through all of life's ups and downs."

237. "I am so grateful for the life we've built together."

238. "You are my forever, and I will cherish you always."

239. "Your love brings me peace, happiness, and fulfillment."

240. "I love how we work together as a team, through thick and thin."

241. "Thank you for being my constant source of love and encouragement."

242. "I appreciate how much you pour into our relationship."

243. "You are my favorite person to share my life with."

244. "Your love gives me strength, and I am forever grateful."

245. "I cherish the way we grow together and continue to love deeply."

246. "You are my heart's home, and I will love you always."

247. "I appreciate the way you support and encourage me every day."

248. "Your love makes my world a better place."

249. "I am so thankful for the love we share and the life we've built."

250. "You are my greatest blessing, and I will never take you for granted."

251. "Your love fills my heart with peace, joy, and contentment."

252. "I love how we make each other better and stronger."

253. "You are the reason my heart feels full of love every day."

254. "I appreciate your unwavering love and support."

255. "Your love is my greatest gift, and I will always cherish it."

256. "I love how we can talk about anything and everything."

257. "You make every moment of life sweeter just by being with me."

258. "I appreciate how you always make time for us, no matter what."

259. "You are my heart's deepest desire, and I love you more every day."

260. "Your love makes me feel like the luckiest person in the world."

261. "I cherish every moment we spend together."

262. "You are the love I never knew I needed, and I am so blessed."

263. "I love how we support each other's dreams and goals."

264. "You make my world brighter and my heart fuller."

265. "Thank you for being the most wonderful partner I could ever ask for."

266. "Your love is my constant, and I will cherish it always."

267. "I appreciate how we grow together, learning from each other every day."

268. "You are my heart's forever love, and I will never take you for granted."

269. "I love how we build each other up and face life together."

270. "You make every day feel special just by being with me."

271. "I appreciate your love, your strength, and your kindness."

272. "You are my greatest blessing, and I will always be thankful for you."

273. "Your love makes everything in life better."

274. "I love how we communicate and support each other through everything."

275. "Thank you for being the person I can always rely on."

276. "I cherish the love we share and the life we've built together."

277. "You are my forever, and I will love you always."

278. "Your love brings me peace, happiness, and fulfillment."

279. "I am so grateful for the way you love and care for me."

280. "I love how we make each other laugh and smile every day."

281. "You are my heart's deepest joy, and I will always love you."

282. "I am so blessed to have a partner who loves me the way you do."

283. "Your love is a constant reminder of how lucky I am."

284. "I love how we continue to grow and deepen our love every day."

285. "You are my greatest gift, and I will treasure you always."

286. "Thank you for loving me through everything, no matter what."

287. "I appreciate all the little things you do to make me feel loved."

288. "You are my heart's greatest treasure, and I am forever grateful."

289. "Your love fills me with happiness, peace, and contentment."

290. "I love how we build each other up and make each other better."

291. "You are my heart's forever love, and I will never stop loving you."

292. "I cherish every moment we spend together."

293. "Thank you for being my partner, my love, and my best friend."

294. "You are the love of my life, and I will always cherish you."

295. "Your love gives me strength, courage, and happiness."

296. "I love how we face life's challenges together and come out stronger."

297. "You are my heart's greatest joy, and I will love you always."

298. "Thank you for loving me, supporting me, and standing by me."

299. "I appreciate the way you make me feel loved and valued."

300. "You are my heart's deepest desire, and I love you more every day."

ENCOURAGEMENT QUOTES AFTER HARDSHIPS

301. "We've been through so much, but I believe our love is stronger because of it."

302. "Even in the hardest times, I know we'll make it through together."

303. "Thank you for standing by my side, even when things weren't easy."

304. "I believe in us, and I believe we can overcome anything together."

305. "No storm is too big for the strength of our love."

306. "We may face challenges, but we'll always come out stronger on the other side."

307. "I'm committed to growing with you, no matter what life throws our way."

308. "Hard times only make me more certain that you are the one I want to spend my life with."

309. "We've faced difficulties, but I trust that our love will keep us moving forward."

310. "I know things have been tough, but I'm so proud of how we've handled it together."

311. "Every challenge we've faced has only deepened my love and respect for you."

312. "I love that we can face adversity as a team, always supporting each other."

313. "We're not perfect, but our love is real and worth fighting for."

314. "Thank you for weathering the storms with me and staying committed to us."

315. "We've come through the fire, and our bond is unbreakable."

316. "No matter how hard it gets, I'm always here with you."

317. "The tough times show me just how much you mean to me."

318. "I'm grateful for your strength and resilience, even in the hardest moments."

319. "Our love is greater than any hardship we face."

320. "We can rebuild and move forward because we have each other."

321. "I'm thankful that even when things are difficult, we choose each other."

322. "Through every trial, I'm reminded of how lucky I am to have you."

323. "I trust that our love is enough to get us through the darkest days."

324. "Thank you for being patient and loving, even when life has been overwhelming."

325. "We've been tested, but we've proven that our love is stronger than any challenge."

326. "I know we've had our struggles, but I still believe in us."

327. "Our love isn't just about the good times; it's about standing together when things get hard."

328. "I love you even more for how we've handled the hard times together."

329. "No matter what, I'm committed to loving you and growing with you."

330. "We've had our share of pain, but I know our love will carry us through."

331. "We've been through so much, but I wouldn't want to go through life with anyone else."

332. "Even in the hardest moments, I know we're building something strong and lasting."

333. "I believe that the struggles we've faced are shaping us into something even more beautiful."

334. "I love how we've stayed resilient and kept loving each other through everything."

335. "Together, we can turn any hardship into an opportunity for growth."

336. "Thank you for never giving up on us, even when things seemed impossible."

337. "The trials we've faced have only proven that our love is unshakable."

338. "I appreciate how you continue to show up for us, even when it's hard."

339. "No matter what we face, I'll always be here, loving and supporting you."

340. "I'm so grateful that we've come out stronger, hand in hand, after everything."

341. "Even in our darkest moments, I've never doubted your love."

342. "Our challenges don't define us; how we rise together does."

343. "We've been through a lot, but it's only made me more sure of our love."

344. "Thank you for loving me through the hardest times. It means the world to me."

345. "We're a team, and together we can face anything life throws at us."

346. "Every hardship has shown me just how resilient and amazing you are."

347. "I love how we've learned and grown through every challenge we've faced."

348. "You've shown incredible strength, and I'm proud to walk this journey with you."

349. "We've been through the fire, and I know we can make it through anything."

350. "Your unwavering love and support have carried me through the toughest moments."

351. "We've come out the other side stronger, and I'm so proud of us."

352. "Even when it's been hard, you've been my rock, and I love you for that."

353. "No matter what comes our way, I know we'll face it together."

354. "Through every storm, I've never lost faith in our love."

355. "We're a living testament to the power of love and perseverance."

356. "I know the journey hasn't been easy, but I wouldn't want to go through it with anyone else."

357. "Your love gives me hope and strength, even in the hardest times."

358. "Thank you for staying with me, even when the road was tough."

359. "We've faced the storms, and our love is still standing strong."

360. "I love how we've come together to overcome everything life has thrown at us."

361. "Our challenges have only made us stronger and more committed to each other."

362. "Through every trial, our love has endured, and I know it always will."

363. "We've faced our share of hardships, but I know we're stronger because of them."

364. "No matter how hard things get, I will always stand by your side."

365. "We've been through it all, and I'm more in love with you today than ever before."

Here is a comprehensive list of 75 resources for married couples that promote Christian love, encompassing books, websites, podcasts, online communities, retreats, and other helpful materials. These resources focus on faith-based relationship guidance, communication, intimacy, conflict resolution, and spiritual growth within marriage.

BOOKS

1. **The Meaning of Marriage** by Timothy Keller
2. **Love & Respect** by Dr. Emerson Eggerichs
3. **Sacred Marriage** by Gary Thomas
4. **The 5 Love Languages** by Gary Chapman
5. **Cherish: The One Word That Changes Everything for Your Marriage** by Gary Thomas
6. **Boundaries in Marriage** by Dr. Henry Cloud & Dr. John Townsend
7. **You and Me Forever** by Francis and Lisa Chan
8. **The Power of a Praying Wife** by Stormie Omartian
9. **The Power of a Praying Husband** by Stormie Omartian
10. **For Women Only** by Shaunti Feldhahn
11. **For Men Only** by Shaunti Feldhahn
12. **His Needs, Her Needs** by Willard F. Harley, Jr.
13. **The Love Dare** by Stephen & Alex Kendrick
14. **Intended for Pleasure** by Ed Wheat & Gaye Wheat
15. **Choosing Marriage** by Debra Fileta
16. **Marriage God's Way** by Scott LaPierre

17. **Two as One: Connecting Daily with Christ and Your Spouse** by Ryan & Selena Frederick

18. **Marriage After God** by Aaron & Jennifer Smith

19. **Praying Together** by Sam and Barbara Hunsberger

20. **Fierce Marriage** by Ryan & Selena Frederick

21. **Crazy Little Thing Called Marriage** by Greg and Erin Smalley

22. **Keep Your Love On! Connection, Communication, and Boundaries** by Danny Silk

23. **Marriage on the Rock** by Jimmy Evans

24. **The Excellent Wife** by Martha Peace

25. **The Exemplary Husband** by Stuart Scott

26. **A Lasting Promise** by Scott Stanley, Daniel Trathen, Savanna McCain, and Milt Bryan

27. **Real Marriage** by Mark and Grace Driscoll

28. **First Years Together: Planning Your Life With Purpose** by Kelsey & Scott Martindale

29. **Vertical Marriage** by Dave and Ann Wilson

30. **The Mingling of Souls** by Matt Chandler

WEBSITES & BLOGS

Heart of Marriage Blog
https://www.heartofmarriageretreat.com/blog
Focus on the Family (www.focusonthefamily.com)
FamilyLife (www.familylife.com)
Fierce Marriage (www.fiercemarriage.com)
The Gottman Institute (www.gottman.com)
Marriage Today (www.marriagetoday.com)

Love and Respect Ministries (www.loveandrespect.com)

Christian Marriage Adventures
(www.christianmarriageadventure.com)

The Unveiled Wife (www.unveiledwife.com)

To Love, Honor, and Vacuum (www.tolovehonorandvacuum.com)

The Marriage Bed (www.themarriagebed.com)

Married and Young (www.marriedandyoung.com)

Marriage 365 (www.marriage365.com)

Engaged Marriage (www.engagedmarriage.com)

Preparing for Marriage (www.preparingformarriage.com)

PODCASTS

The Fierce Marriage Podcast by Ryan & Selena Frederick

Focus on Marriage Podcast by Focus on the Family

FamilyLife Today by FamilyLife

Marriage After God Podcast by Aaron & Jennifer Smith

The Naked Marriage Podcast by Dave & Ashley Willis

Love and Respect Podcast by Dr. Emerson Eggerichs

The Christian Marriage Coach Podcast by Dale and Veronica Partridge

One Extraordinary Marriage Podcast by Tony & Alisa DiLorenzo

MarriageToday Podcast by Jimmy & Karen Evans

SavvySauce Podcast (Christian insights into marriage)

Awesome Marriage Podcast by Dr. Kim Kimberling

The Fierce Marriage Podcast by Fierce Marriage

The Real Marriage Podcast by Mark & Grace Driscoll

RETREATS & CONFERENCES

Heart of Marriage Retreat
https://www.heartofmarriageretreat.com/details
Weekend to Remember by FamilyLife
(www.familylife.com/weekend-to-remember)
Marriage Encounter (www.marriageencounter.org)
Fierce Marriage Getaways by Ryan & Selena Frederick
(www.fiercemarriage.com)
Marriage Retreats by Focus on the Family
(www.focusonthefamily.com/marriage/marriage-retreats)
Christian Marriage Adventures Retreats
(www.christianmarriageadventure.com/marriage-retreats)
Marriage Today Retreats (www.marriagetoday.com/retreats)
Living in Love Retreats (www.livinginlove.org)

ONLINE COMMUNITIES & FORUMS

The Passion Pathway Community (Our private community for
program participants)
The Unveiled Wife Community
(www.unveiledwife.com/community)
Christian Marriage Adventures Facebook Group (Search
"Christian Marriage Adventure" on Facebook)
Fierce Marriage Community
(www.fiercemarriage.com/community)

These resources provide a mix of inspiration, biblical wisdom, and practical tools for strengthening Christian marriages. Whether you're looking for something to read, listen to, or attend in person, there's something here for every couple at every stage of their journey.

REFERENCES

Chapman, G. (2015). The 5 love languages: The secret to love that lasts. Northfield Publishing.

Cloud, H., & Townsend, J. (2012). Boundaries in marriage. Zondervan.

Dobson, J. (2014). Love for a lifetime: Building a marriage that will go the distance. Multnomah.

Eggerichs, E. (2004). Love and respect: The love she most desires; the respect he desperately needs. Thomas Nelson.

Feldhahn, S. (2013). The surprising secrets of highly happy marriages: The little things that make a big difference. Multnomah Books.

Gottman, J. M., & Silver, N. (2015). The seven principles for making marriage work: A practical guide from the country's foremost relationship expert. Harmony.

Keller, T., & Keller, K. (2011). The meaning of marriage: Facing the complexities of commitment with the wisdom of God. Penguin Books.

LaHaye, T., & LaHaye, B. (2000). The act of marriage: The beauty of sexual love. Zondervan.

Parrott, L., & Parrott, L. (2016). Saving your marriage before it starts: Seven questions to ask before--and after--you marry. Zondervan.

Thomas, G. (2000). Sacred marriage: What if God designed marriage to make us holy more than to make us happy? Zondervan.

ABOUT THE AUTHOR:

Danny and Amelia Coles' journey to oneness began in 1985. After a chance encounter at work, their relationship began. Following six months of dating and another six months of engagement, Danny and Amelia married in April of 1986 and started on the road to becoming one in marriage. Envision the electrifying synergy sparked when you blend the wisdom of a seasoned pastor with over 30 years of dedicated marriage ministry alongside the dynamic insights of an educator with an extensive tenure on a bustling college campus. Add to this potent mix a thriving marriage, passionately devoted to nurturing others through their deep expertise in marriage ministry. Together, they ignite a transformative force, combining decades of experience to inspire and guide with unparalleled zeal and expertise, motivating you to embark on your own transformative journey. As a result, Danny and Amelia have formed the Marriage Oneness Institute to empower kingdom-minded couples on a journey to rediscover intimacy and strengthen their relationship. In the Passion Pathway Program, they teach a 6-week online course to rekindle your love and deepen your connection.

For more information, please visit https://www.dannyamelia.org/

Made in the USA
Columbia, SC
22 November 2024

47023918R00074